Think
Yourself
Successful

REWIRE YOUR MIND,
BECOME CONFIDENT, AND
ACHIEVE YOUR GOALS

Alireza Azmandian, Ph.D.

New York   Chicago   San Francisco   Lisbon   London   Madrid   Mexico City
Milan   New Delhi   San Juan   Seoul   Singapore   Sydney   Toronto

Library of Congress Cataloging-in-Publication Data

Azmandian, Alireza.
    Think yourself successful : rewire your mind, become confident, and achieve your goals / by Alireza Azmandian.
        p.   cm.
    Includes bibliographical references.
    ISBN-13: 978-0-07-174124-8
    ISBN-10: 0-07-174124-0
    1. Success.   2. Self-actualization (Psychology).   I. Title.

BF637.S8A958   2010
158.1—dc22   2009051805

1 2 3 4 5 6 7 8 9 10 11 12 13 14 15 16   WFR/WFR   1 9 8 7 6 5 4 3 2 1 0

ISBN 978-0-07-174124-8
MHID   0-07-174124-0

McGraw-Hill books are available at special quantity discounts to use as premiums and sales promotions or for use in corporate training programs. To contact a representative, please e-mail us at bulksales@mcgraw-hill.com.

CONTENTS

PREFACE

*I*f beliefs and ways of thinking have such an important role in a person's life, if all of your accomplishments in this world and the hereafter hinge on your thoughts and views, if wealth or poverty, health or illness, success or failure, happening or not happening all depend on how a person thinks, then the important question is: "How should we think?"

How can we think positively? How can the way we think attract wealth? How should we think so that we achieve whatever we want in life and make our future more beautiful?

The answer to these questions is a phenomenon that is one of mankind's triumphs in the twenty-first century. It is an intelligent and systematic outlook on and approach to the thought process, called the "Technology of Thought." Through this method, we are able to create a comprehensive system within ourselves so that we can always think beautifully, positively, creatively, ambitiously, and optimistically and create whatever we desire.

The Technology of Thought is a scientific and innovative system opening doorways of opportunity through which we arrive at an ideal world, a new reality. In this new world, whatever you imagine, you create. Everything is different for you in this paradise. By using the Technology of Thought, all of creation is at your beck and call. Whatever you say (think), will happen. Whatever you desire, will come to fruition. Whatever you destine to happen, will happen.

Every one of your thoughts is like a musical note that is played in the world, and the entire universe has the responsibility to harmonize with your thought-note, to ultimately create the symphony of your life. Therefore, when you play a beautiful, positive, and ambitious note, all of creation will harmonize with it, and you will experience bliss each and every second of your life.

When your state of mind is one of complete despair and pessimism, however, you think negatively, and it's ultimately this mindset that will conduct the orchestra of your life. The universe will also join in this sad symphony, causing failure and defeat. But when you think beautifully, everything will become beautiful for you. Ultimately, through the Technology of Thought, you *can* think yourself successful.

ACKNOWLEDGMENTS AND DEDICATION

*T*hanks to the Compassionate Lord, who has allowed me to learn beautifully and live wonderfully. He has made this book a means for me to teach others that they can live differently and amazingly.

My deepest gratitude to my daughter, Dr. Fatemeh Azmandian, for her assistance in translating and editing this book. I would also like to extend my sincerest thanks to my son, Mahdi Azmandian, for his hard work and commitment in editing the book. And to my wife, Dr. Azam Bakhtiarian, who, with love and support, stood beside me and created the means to achieve transformation and wisdom.

I dedicate this book to all of my teachers and instructors who taught me how to improve the quality of my life. Thanks to Dr. Wayne Dyer, Jim Rohn, Anthony Robbins, Marshall Silver, Brian Tracy, and other motivational speakers who inspired me and from whom I learned a lot.

My most heartfelt thanks to John Aherne from McGraw-Hill, for inspiring me to translate my book into English. I never would have had this opportunity were it not for you.

And to the people who envision the greatness of our society and who believe that to make progress, it is necessary to transform the thoughts and beliefs of each and every one of us.

And to all the people of the world, with the hope that together, with new thoughts, great beliefs, and endless effort, we can create a new world, a better place to live in the twenty-first century.

I dedicate this book to anyone, anywhere in the world, who, by using the principles of the Technology of Thought, aims to think beautifully and create an even more beautiful life.

INTRODUCTION

*H*uman beings have so much hidden potential within them. Only a small fraction and tiny, incipient nuggets of this infinite treasure have been discovered. People have yet to discover the unlimited ability and power they possess. Whatever we think, we create; and whatever we desire, we achieve. In such a world, no obstacles exist. It is a world filled with opportunities, and each opportunity can be turned into a source of wealth. Wealth is not limited to money; rather, all of our positive achievements can be considered wealth. Knowledge is a kind of wealth, as are love and happiness. Having strong relationships are aspects of wealth. A deep connection with the spiritual world is also considered wealth. In the new world that is created by the principles of the Technology of Thought, everything can be different.

WHAT IS THE TECHNOLOGY
OF THOUGHT?

The Technology of Thought is a phenomenon whereby we change the way we think in order to achieve greater confidence, fulfillment, and success. In my years of research, I came to realize that by understanding and programming our subconscious minds, we can create an internal movement within ourselves and completely modify all of our negative mental, emotional, and personal characteristics. By creating a transformation and altering our belief system—by changing the fundamental way we think—we can become a "whole new person," one who always thinks positively and creates beautifully.

The year was 1983. I had been working for the Iranian television broadcasting station for four years and was making a couple hundred dollars a month. My first child, Fatemeh, had just been born, and we were living under extremely difficult conditions. I was paying a mortgage on a very modest home I had purchased in a shabby neighborhood in Tehran. When I was a child, I had big dreams and had gone to great lengths to achieve them, but I still felt unsuccessful. Even though I had always wanted to pursue levels of education beyond the undergraduate degree, I never thought it was a possibility, and I became caught up in the daily challenges of life.

One day the Iranian television broadcasting station sent me on an all-expense-paid trip to the holy city of Mecca as a reward. As part of the Hajj pilgrimage,[1] I set out on a spiritual journey. The day I touched the black stone near the Kaabah,[2] which felt as though I was shaking hands with God and greeting Him, I asked that He transform my life—to move me past a life of exhaustion, discontentment, and defeat and to make me successful, so that I could live my life differently.

Eventually, this spiritual and divine journey came to an end and I returned to Iran, all the while not knowing how my requests were materializing in the real world. I knew that He was the Initiator of all things and that something had to happen. Only a few days had passed when a friend, who had come to Iran from the United States, visited me and as a gift gave me the book *Think and Grow Rich* by Napoleon Hill. This self-help book was written in English and had not yet been translated into Persian. I stared at it in wonder and thought, "Could it really be possible to think and achieve all your goals?" At the time, I did not know that He had answered my prayers to guide me onto another path. He had arranged this book to be a tool for my transformation.

I read the book with great enthusiasm, and it changed the way I looked at the world. That book sent me a message: "By no means are you condemned to this kind of life. You can pursue a higher education in any field that you want, at the best universities in the world. You can achieve wealth. You can attain a world of spirituality, knowledge, and piety. Stand up and make a resolution. Make a decision and know that life is full of opportunities and you can transform opportunities into sources of wealth for yourself. You can live and take pleasure in it."

This divine message changed everything for me. At that very moment, I stood up and made the resolution to transform. I said to myself, "I should get up and start my life anew and remove this pain in my heart."[3] It was as though the universe was waiting for me to make such a decision and resolution so that, upon my command, it could take action and arrange the means to create a great transformation and success. Indeed, everything changed, without me even knowing it.

Two years later in 1985, after making living arrangements and with some money that I had saved, I traveled to the United States with my wife and three-year-old daughter, Fatemeh. My goal was to continue my divine mission and to study, research, and teach in the best universities in America, to gain experiences so that I might return to my country bearing gifts and share what I'd learned with my fellow countrymen, so that their lives could become beautiful like mine—even better than mine—and so they could know that, indeed, it is possible to live differently and create a magnificent world for oneself.

After twelve years of living, researching, and teaching in American universities and traveling to more than fifty countries around the world, I returned to Iran to begin another mission. While teaching at the engineering department of Tehran University in the field of industrial engineering, I held novel and groundbreaking educational seminars on the Technology of Thought for various groups of people, including students, university professors, teachers, business professionals, and other influential members of society. Thus began the implementation of a movement for the seventy million people of Iran.

By executing the principles found in the Technology of Thought, I set out to transform thoughts and belief systems to create a whole new Iran—an Iran with millions of loving, intelligent, spiritual, wealthy, and peaceful individuals with high character, self-confidence, and exceptional people skills, who shine in the arena of life and take advantage of every blessing and enjoy each and every moment of their life. And now, I want to share this transformation with you.

ROAD MAP TO *THINK YOURSELF SUCCESSFUL*

Think Yourself Successful reveals infinite possibilities that lay before you. You, too, can become a successful, flourishing individual who has become transformed by the principles of the Technology of Thought. Once transformed, you will find the path of excellence, and this book tells you how to travel down this path, how to think, and how to succeed, step by step, toward the life you want. Here is what you will discover in the pages ahead:

- The first chapter of the book tells the story of how coming from poverty, I was able to go to the United States, the land of opportunity, and how I achieved success through the Technology of Thought.
- Chapter 2 introduces the basic concepts of the Technology of Thought and explains how by programming your subconscious mind, you can instill new beliefs and a great attitude about yourself. This way, you can inspire beautiful thoughts and ideas, bringing you closer to the life you want.
- Chapter 3 describes how our subconscious mind works and how you can reprogram yours to achieve success. Through the law of attraction, you can draw in success from the universe and accomplish your goals.
- Chapter 4 explains how, through the Technology of Thought, you can manage your feelings and state of mind to achieve serenity and internal peace.
- Chapter 5 reveals the thirty principles necessary to achieve self-confidence and allow you to establish positive character traits to obtain self-esteem. These

thirty principles of self-confidence send powerful signals to your subconscious mind.

- Chapter 6 explains how communication and human relationships are the golden keys to success. Eighty-five percent of life's achievements are attained through the way we communicate with others. This chapter shows how we can develop real and authentic relationships with other people to attract success.
- Chapter 7 shows you how to set goals at work and in life. By using the laws of nature, we can accomplish our goals.
- Chapter 8 shows you how to be resilient and avoid some of life's greatest challenges. I'll show you how to stand firm in the face of problems, giving you ways to solve them and achieve success and inner peace.
- Chapter 9 will show you how to transform yourself and make permanent changes in your life.
- Chapter 10 discusses how you can become wealthy and financially successful.

And in the final chapter of the book, I will share a letter with you conveying my final message of encouragement and positive affirmations.

I hope that you read this book with an open mind and believe that it can alter your destiny in the same way *Think and Grow Rich* by Napoleon Hill changed my destiny. Were it not for that book, I would not be where I am today. Use this book as an instrument for your own transformation.

Think Yourself Successful is different from all the other books that you have read up until now. This is not just a book, but a collection of instructions that, in fact, reveal the secret to the power that you possess to create your own destiny. Think of this book as a tool to guide you onto the path to a successful life, giving you clarity to discover who you are, where you are, what you are living for, and where you are going.

You will learn how to harness positive power to change the way you think, become more confident, and achieve your personal goals. Once all of these things are in place, you will experience tranquility, joy, and contentment. Use the principles in the pages ahead to build your attractive and successful future filled with meaningful relationships. You will discover your own greatness and bask in the wonderful feeling of self-confidence and self-assurance.

Think Yourself Successful holds within it the great secrets to a beautiful life and the secrets to success, happiness, and the path to serenity and healthy living. However, to achieve all of this requires one condition: that you put all of the techniques and methods within this book into action and continually exercise all the principles of the Technology of Thought. Remember that knowledge and awareness without action will have no impact, so I ask you with enthusiasm and encouragement to use this information and patiently act on it to create your masterpiece—your life.

This book is a culmination of a lifetime of research, as I unrelentingly explored the valley of existence and traveled to more than fifty countries in search of a better way to live and achieve excellence. With my exploration, I discovered endless treasure and marked the path to this treasure with a map. This book is that map—reap the benefits of this gift, for it is yours to claim. I wish you good luck on the path of happiness and success!

1

A NEW MISSION

*I*t was 10 A.M. on a weekend morning. Twelve very productive years in America had passed, eight of which were spent in Los Angeles and the other four in New York City. At the time, I was living on the twenty-first floor of a fifty-story building in New York that overlooked the Atlantic Ocean. I sat beside a window facing the sea, watching the sailboats pass by, lost in my thoughts.

I thought to myself, "What a world! My, how these people enjoy their lives!" Then I took a look inside my apartment. A maid was busy cleaning, trying hard to do a good job so that we would be satisfied with her work and continue to employ her in the coming weeks and give her money to take care of her family in a foreign land. This was because she, too, had come from another country for a better life. In another part of the city, poverty was running rampant. I remembered seeing a group of people who did not even have a home to call their own. They would sleep out on the streets, and throughout the day, they would beg for money at intersections from people who were driving fancy cars. New York was indeed diverse, with all kinds of people living in this city of soaring skyscrapers—a city rich with culture, the arts, films, plays, and theater. New York is the heart of the national economy, a city of money and politics.

I was reminded of a time about twelve years ago. It was a beautiful autumn evening when, after receiving visas for the United States, I flew from Iran to Los Angeles, accompanied by my wife and three-year-old daughter. We made our first stop in New York. We were supposed to fly from New York to Los Angeles a couple of hours later, but we were delayed at the passport and security check for so long that we missed our connecting flight. The airline was obliged to provide hotel accommodations so that we could catch the next flight to Los Angeles, which was the following day.

We felt like strangers exploring a whole new world. At 8 P.M., a lovely suite was prepared at a beautiful hotel in New York City for an Iranian family of three who had just begun an unforgettable journey, a journey to achieve our dreams of a higher education and to utilize the concept of *Think and Grow Rich*.[1]

WHAT A DIFFERENCE TWO NIGHTS MAKE!

That night I couldn't sleep; I was immersed in my thoughts, thinking "Lord, look at where I stand now!" and "What are your future plans for us?" It had all started with the book *Think and Grow Rich* by Napoleon Hill. Were it not for this book, instead of being in New York that night, I would have been in my cramped sixty-square-meter apartment in a shabby neighborhood in Tehran, concerned with how early I would have to wake up the next morning to go stand in line to buy my daughter, Fatemeh, some government-subsidized milk.[2] These scattered thoughts didn't allow me a moment's reprieve. In the middle of the night, I gazed out my hotel window into the streets of New York and started thinking about my past.

I remembered the day when I was six years old and my mother gave me a coin and said, "Alireza, with this money buy some grapes so that tonight we may all dine on bread and grapes." There were six of us along with our mother and father and grandmother, for a total of nine people living in a ten-square-meter rented studio. The meager wages that my father earned were barely enough to pay the rent and buy some bread, so for a six-year-old child, the promise of bread and grapes for dinner was glad tidings. I took the coin from my mother and walked through the streets of our poor neighborhood until I reached the grocery store around the corner. The exquisite grape vines that sparkled under the bright lights grabbed my attention. I enthusiastically approached the man in charge, gave him the coin, and said, "Sir, please give me these grapes." The man half glanced at my measly coin, threw it back at me, and said, "Get out of here, kid. You can't buy any grapes with this!" I was sad, thinking, "No bread and grapes for dinner tonight."

But then a box caught my eye, one in which the man had thrown damaged grapes that he was discarding. I asked him, "Sir, can you please give me some of those grapes?" I suppose the man felt sorry for me. He accepted my money and threw some of the damaged grapes into a paper bag and handed it to me. Delighted, I brought the grapes home for my mother to wash, and yes, we dined on bread and grapes that night. That night also left a huge question mark burned into the mind of this six-year-old child: "Why? Why couldn't we eat bread and grapes like other people?" At that moment, despite my young age, my parents' poverty hit me more than ever, leading me to ask myself, "God, what must I do to not end up living in poverty like my mother and father?"

While sitting on the bed in the hotel and gazing out the window at the comings and goings of people in the streets of New York, and after having a delicious meal with my wife and daughter, I thought to myself, "What has transpired between these two dinners and these two nights? How can a person move on from a world of poverty and deprivation to one of great achievement?

"Are humans doomed to their fate, or is their fate in their own hands? What causes the difference between poverty and wealth? What separates success from failure? How can we make the most of our blessings and enjoy every single moment of life? How can one think about success and make it happen?" These thoughts left me unsettled, and from the top of the hotel I wanted to observe the vast sky, think of my life in Iran, and reflect on the past, so that I could truly enjoy the present and plan a more beautiful future. Yes, the sky was the limit!

As I continued to reflect upon how far I had come from the six-year-old boy in search of a good meal, suddenly, a map of Iran on the television screen on CNN caught my attention. Turning up the volume, I saw that the network was looking back and analyzing the hostage situation that occurred in Iran during 1981 and Iraq's war against Iran, which had begun six years earlier, describing the incomprehensible loss caused by it.

Watching these images in a foreign land, I was flooded with memories of my six years at the frontlines of the war and my television and radio reporting for the Islamic Republic of Iran Broadcasting station (known as the IRIB).

There I reported on the bravery of Iranian soldiers in a battle between good and evil, witnessing with my own eyes the demise of my countrymen throughout the six years of war, an experience that left me filled with sorrow. I used the following sentence from the Quran to console myself: "Lord, I accept your will and I obey your command and I am content with what you have bestowed upon me; I have no God but you."

TIMES OF WAR: SHAPING THE PATH OF LIFE

I was a reporter for the political, economic, and industrial division of the IRIB for six years. Even though I had no prior experience in news and reporting, the sheer thrill and exhilaration of the revolution kept me working almost twenty-four hours a day at the IRIB. My responsibilities ranged from inspecting war footage to television reporting, none of which really had anything to do with my field, which was mechanical engineering. Nevertheless, they say that an engineering and mathematical mind prepares one for success in any of life's arenas. My life as a reporter boosted my self-confidence and made it possible for me to stand out at the IRIB, and so I was later assigned to the president's office, reporting news related to his presidency.

Narrating history, when in the midst of it, has special significance. As a reporter for the president's office, for a country that had just gone through a revolution and was experiencing many dramatic events, I conveyed news for people with as much clarity as I could. At the time, there were only two television channels, and each would broadcast for only a few hours at night.

Channel One had an important mission, especially its news division: to report news about the ongoing revolution. Whoever had a television at home would watch Channel One, and the next day, the subject of everyone's conversation revolved around analysis of the news and television broadcasts.

After Operation Eagle Claw (the failed hostage rescue attempt by the U.S. military in 1980), I was the first and only reporter to be immediately dispatched, in a five-passenger plane and military helicopter, to the site of the accident in the desert of Tabas.

The sight of the American soldiers and the remnants of the helicopters in the middle of the desert was very solemn. I prepared a television exclusive on the incident that the whole world was waiting to see. That night people around the nation, and around the world via satellite, shocked by the attack of American planes, saw me on their television screens reporting from the site of the accident in the desert of Tabas.

On September 22, 1980, the Iraqi war against Iran
began with the attack on Iran's airports by Iraqi planes.
The president's quarters were filled with terror. The Iranian president, Abolhassan Banisadr, undoubtedly had no
military or combat experience, but as the commander in
chief, he was in charge. Unfortunately, he was so involved
in politics and faction disputes that he was not able to
play a deciding role in the war. The only true leadership
came from Imam Khomeini, who was able to give hope to
a nation that had never seen war and to rally the troops
toward the fronts to form a human barricade against the
assault by Saddam Hussein.

The headquarters of the presidency was transferred
from the presidential office to the army command base,
and as the reporter assigned to the president, I followed
Banisadr into the command room of the base and began
reporting the news and documenting the war.

The city of Khorramshahr fell, and Saddam announced
that he had taken possession of a large piece of Iranian soil,
equivalent to the size of the entire country of Lebanon.
The IRIB did not inform people of all that was happening
during the war, many circumstances of which were very
upsetting; but since I knew the true nature of the situation,
I endured many hardships during those times.

Every day, the president, accompanied by the top
military leaders, would visit the various command bases
in order to rally the troops and see them off to battle. I

witnessed everything as it happened. I remember how the soldiers at the Gazvin command base were so despondent that only a religious power could lift their spirits. Banisadr's speeches were not enough to encourage the military personnel (who were each dealing with their own issues), and, adding to the desperation, the base commanders would periodically report on equipment failures.

We flew from Gazvin to Hamedan and from there to the airbase in Dezfool. Despite the risk, we had no other choice, and so with Iranian fighter planes as escort, under the cover of night we reached the skies over Dezfool, only steps from the battlefields. The Dezfool command base was pitch dark and under code red. That night we met with the Iranian fighter pilots, who used their planes to hunt down Iraqi tanks and prevent their advance. A large group of their comrades had recently been the victims of an enemy airstrike, leaving the majority of them martyrs of this imposed war. Maybe there was no other choice. We had no equipped and operational military forces on the ground to ward off the tanks, so the bomb-dropping fighter planes of the air force were the only glimmer of hope on a battlefield full of despair.

When broadcasting the news and military reports, we were especially careful not to include the slightest whiff of desperation or of conflict between the heads of state. We would emphasize the small victories of the army so as to instill hope in the hearts of the people.

Along with the president; the air force commander, General Fakoori; the head of army headquarters, General Falahi; and the commander of the ground forces, General Zahirnejad, we surveyed the battlefields in the south. At the beginning of the war, the battle statistics were very discouraging. There wasn't much of a chance against Iraqi forces. We went to the Karkhe battlefields and came upon a group of soldiers weeping in despair. Witnessing such a sight was completely devastating.

In the middle of the night, I left the president in Ahvaz and took a group of cameramen in my charge through a detour to Abadan, which was surrounded by enemy forces. Most of the people had fled the city, and only the army, volunteer units, troops, and a few guerrilla fighters remained. The missile attacks on Abadan from the other side of the barricade were relentless. We stayed at one of the abandoned hotels of the city that served as a command post for the volunteer units. The terrifying sound of bullets blasting into buildings and through different parts of the city deprived us of even a moment's rest. The hotel building was at risk of being destroyed at any moment.

There was nothing we could do. We had to wait until the light of day to obtain an account of the events in Abadan, a city we had long known for its beauty, the city of Iran's oil company. In the black of night, the only blazes of light were from the flames of the oil refinery storage tanks, which lit up the city. Seeing the refineries, a massive national resource, up in flames left this dedicated Iranian reporter's heart in pain. I thought, "God, what is this place? Where are we now? What must we do? Why are we in the midst of such a war?"

It was toward the end of March, in the middle of the night, when a group of IRIB cameramen and I arrived at the frontlines, a few days before Operation Baytul Mogaddas began. The primary objective of this operation was to liberate Khorramshahr. There were moments of horror and flashes of hope for the liberation of the city that had been nicknamed "The City of Blood." The operation began following prayers at the command base and the commanders' last-minute discussion of strategy and tactics. The plan was to launch a massive attack on the Iraqis from three battlefronts simultaneously.

The beginning of the mission was a near-defeat with much loss, but it was imperative that Khorramshahr be liberated. The operation lasted two months. Finally, in a brave and ingeniously designed attack, the Iraqis were surrounded, and at dawn on May 24, we entered the city of Khorramshahr with our devoted soldiers. The Iraqis were so caught off guard that for hours not one bullet was fired from the Iraqi camps. Iraqi soldiers by the thousands were taken prisoner.

I was the first reporter to enter the city with the soldiers. The handful of remaining soldiers of the Khorramshahr army, who had lost their friends and loved ones, entered Khorramshahr ahead of everyone else. They headed straight for Jameh Mosque, which had been turned to rubble. In front of the Khorramshahr Jameh Mosque, I witnessed images that I will never forget. The remaining Khorramshahr soldiers, overcome with emotion, kissed the floor, doors, and walls of the mosque and cried. A mix of joy and sorrow over the death of their loved ones filled the air of the shattered mosque. They had returned home, a home that had been left in ruins.

THE DAWN OF A NEW LIFE

It was nearing sunrise. Before my morning prayer, I took another glance at the streets of New York from my hotel room—I was in a new world. Accompanied by my wife and daughter, I went downstairs to eat breakfast. Later that day, I took a stroll in front of the hotel while waiting for the cab that was to take us to the airport. For me, these were moments of beauty. Certainly, after times of difficulty there must come periods of relief. This is one of the laws of nature, for those who decide to do something about their life alter their *own* destiny. I thought to myself, why don't most people put any effort toward improving the quality of their life? Why do most people get caught up in daily struggles and find themselves constantly overcome with worry?

Then again, there are certain people who choose to take a different course of action in life and achieve a world of success. The difference between ignorance and awareness is essentially what separates failure from success. Some people live in a state of ignorance and never analyze or evaluate their life. They do not know *who* they are and *what* they are doing. They do not *see* opportunities, let alone seize them. They do not realize life's treasures. They constantly complain and talk pessimistically. These people have unflattering characteristics. They always think about life's hardships and failures and focus on the negative. They constantly ask "Why?" "Why is the economy so bad? Why are the prices so high? Why doesn't anyone love me? Why am I never successful at anything? Why does everything bad in the world happen to me? Why do I have such bad luck?"

Indeed, the questions you ask yourself determine the quality of your life. The exquisite lives of successful people are made from their own will.

It is worth mentioning that from the point of view of the Technology of Thought, there are two connotations for the word *why*. On the one hand, there is the aforementioned complaint-filled form of the word; and on the other hand, there is also a robust *why* used in seeking the unknown. In the coming chapters, there will be further discussion on "The Power of *Why*." This has been an introduction to how words affect the subconscious mind, a topic that we will discuss in greater detail later on. We shall describe how words like *why* originate from a corrupted soul, and in fact continue to corrupt the soul, and how the word *how* stems from a healthy soul and is nourishing. Indeed, successful people are those who are consistently aware of all things, including the words they use.

It is 8 A.M. on October 6, 1985. We stroll down the street near our hotel in New York City. It is a lovely autumn morning in a country they call the "Land of Opportunity." The fresh raindrops have added a special softness to the morning air. Cars pass by as they carry their owners to work. This is a world of people who strive to earn a living. Surely, the result of effort and commitment is success. As it is written in the Quran, "Everything is achieved through effort."

We return to the hotel and see the driver, sent by our airline, waiting for us. We get into a minivan and on this beautiful, historic day, we cruise through the streets of Manhattan until we arrive at JFK Airport. I glance over at the innocent face of my daughter, Fatemeh, who is taking a journey in the steps of her father to a land different—far different—from her own to arrive at a world of beauty and success. I look over at my wife's face and she is content.

Tap into Your Thoughts

People who are self-aware continually ask themselves, "Who am I?" "Where am I?" and "What am I doing?" Self-aware and successful people constantly evaluate their life and focus on its beauty and positive aspects. Instead of asking "Why?" which is a complaint-riddled question, they ask "How?" This new way of thinking is one of the keys to success.

Content and grateful for what they have, they ask, "How can I improve the quality of my life? How can I succeed in this situation? How can I achieve complete health? How can I make stronger connections with others? How is it possible that God loves me so? How can I improve my luck? How . . . ? How . . . ? How . . . ?"

The word *why* closes the doors of opportunity. It shows ungratefulness, which wipes away the good fortune from your life. But the word *how* conveys gratitude, which gives way to infinite good fortune.

Her grin is a testament to the beginning of a new chapter in the life of a woman—a mother—whose thirty-one-year-old husband, inspired by Napoleon Hill, has changed his belief system and has decided to create a beautiful existence for himself and his family.

As we sit back, relaxed in the car, the streets and sky-scrapers pass by us: gorgeous cars, beautiful buildings; but not far away, the homeless, some drug-addicted, are lying along the sidewalk. Some parts of New York are danger-ous, and wherever there is poverty, corruption is not too far behind.

SIX HOURS OF THOUGHT, SIX HOURS OF IDEAS FLYING THROUGH MY MIND

We arrive at JFK Airport. From there, we board a Pan American jumbo jet to take us from New York to our final destination of Los Angeles. The flight takes a total of six hours to travel from the East Coast to the West Coast. During those six hours we spent in the skies over the United States, a myriad of ideas raced through my mind. We were embarking on a journey toward a future that would be completely different from our past. This is what it means to make a *transformation* in one's life. When we transform, and consciously align ourselves with the laws of nature, everything changes for us. Time and space and all of creation bow to our will and bring forth all of the opportunities in the world in favor of fulfilling the goals of a true believer.

Throughout the six-hour flight, as Fatemeh was play-ing with the toy given to her by the kind, cheerful flight attendant and as her mother was entertained by the different in-flight programs, I humbly thought to myself, "Lord, you have truly blessed me and my family and have opened a new chapter in our lives."

I always wanted to continue my studies and achieve the highest degree of education, pursuing my goal of becoming a scholar who can make a difference in the world. I hoped to walk the path of greatness, ascend, and reach God in a spiritual sense. I decided to make a change in my life. These moments spent in the friendly skies were glad tidings of the fulfillment of my dreams. Yes, the sky *is* the limit.

The enormous airplane continued to soar through the skies at high speed, just like my thoughts of my past, present, and future. I believe that essentially, a person's entire world is shaped by his or her thoughts and that every single thought has a consequence.

YOUR THOUGHTS ORCHESTRATE YOUR LIFE'S SYMPHONY

A beautiful and positive thought creates a new world in one's life. Whatever we think, we create. Our existence is all about thoughts, which all lead to creation; think and you shall create. Whatever reality people create begins as a thought in their head. A person's life is the result of his or her every single thought. What separates individuals from one another are the kinds of thoughts they have. The difference between a successful person and one who has

Tap into Your Thoughts

Each and every one of your thoughts is as a note played in the universe, and all of creation must respond to your note and play in the same key (whether positive or negative) so that ultimately, your "Life's Symphony" is created. If your thoughts are beautiful, positive, goal-oriented, and hopeful, the entire universe will play beautifully and create a masterpiece from your Life's Symphony—the quality of your life depends on the quality of your thoughts.

failed is the difference in their belief and thought system. Poverty and failure is the result of poor thoughts, and wealth and success is the result of rich thoughts. You are what you believe.

It doesn't matter if you think that you will succeed or think that you will fail; in both cases you've thought right. If you think you will succeed, your positive thoughts will move and guide you toward success. If from the very beginning you think that you will fail, feeling negative, you will either give up or your behavior and actions will cause you to fail.

Your thoughts are powerful and can bring about health, just as they can cause illness. People who have beautiful and hopeful thoughts stay healthy. People who have negative and cynical thoughts not only face failure in life, but they also attract health problems.

YOUR MIND IS A THOUGHT-GENERATING FACTORY

Your mind is like a factory; it is responsible for generating your thoughts at every moment. On average, each human conceives about sixty thousand thoughts a day, and these thoughts are what shapes one's life. Thoughts take form in the world of realities.

Thoughts can transform into wealth; and a thought can even bring peace of mind or lead to anxiety and depression. Thoughts generate self-confidence and self-esteem. Thoughts are what induce either feelings of love or feelings of hatred. Thoughts create either friendships or enemies. Thoughts produce either happiness or sorrow. Thoughts bring about either success or failure. Thoughts lead to either virtue or vice. Thoughts are a beautiful sea of wholeness. (One hour of brilliant thinking is equivalent to seventy years of worship at the Gracious Lord's altar, according to Islamic thought.)

Humans plant the seeds of their thoughts in this land of existence, and they reap what they sow in the form of their life's achievements.

Tap into Your Thoughts

Tell me how you think and I will tell you what kind of a person you are.

Tell me how you think and I will tell you how rich you will be in the future.

Tell me how you think and I will tell you what level of education and degree of higher learning you *have* obtained and *will* obtain.

Tell me how you think and I will tell you how much mental and spiritual peace you possess.

Tell me how you think and I will tell you how you sleep at night.

Tell me how you think and I will tell you what the future holds for you.

Tell me how you think and I will tell you how many friends and how many enemies you have.

Tell me how you think and I will tell you what others think of you.

Tell me how you think and I will tell you how healthy you are.

Indeed, your life is shaped by the quality of your individual thoughts. A person's quality of life is determined by the quality of his each and every thought.

As we flew to Los Angeles, I thought to myself, "There are four hundred passengers on this plane, each busy with his or her own matters and creating individual thoughts and ideas." That is great for those passengers who were thinking beautiful thoughts, thoughts such as hope, faith in something greater than themselves, faith in themselves, faith in life, faith in the future, faith in creating an amazing tomorrow, faith in success. It is with these thoughts that they have become successful.

On the other hand, somewhere on this plane could be a pessimistic soul thinking, "What if this plane doesn't safely arrive at its destination? What if it crashes? What if . . . ? What if . . . ? What if . . . ?" That person turns the six-hour flight from what could have been an enjoyable and pleasant experience to one filled with anxiety and stress. Indeed, the quality of every single thought determines whether the individual is filled with tranquility or worry.

Throughout the flight, the passengers are taken care of by cheerful flight attendants. While enjoying various entertaining, funny, and heartwarming movies, the passengers create beautiful moments for themselves. During this time, the captain announces that he has begun his descent for landing at the Los Angeles airport. We fastened our seatbelts and prepared for landing. Everything was so lovely and wondrous, knowing that these beautiful moments would result in the creation of a wonderful future and the attainment of knowledge and greatness.

If someone had asked me why I came to the United States, I would have said that I wanted to see for myself how you can *think and grow rich*, think and become a scholar, think and become pious and spiritual, think and obtain all of life's magnificent achievements, and think and connect with God.

I wanted to see for myself what the idea of self-management was all about. We didn't come to the United States just for the comfort and dazzling sights that it had to offer. We didn't come for the highways or the skyscrapers. We came here to, in the words of the Prophet Muhammad, "Seek knowledge, even if it requires travelling to China [the ends of the earth]."

We came to understand the power of human potential, how we can bridge the distance between how we live and how we should live, the distance between failure and success, illness and health, ugliness and beauty, doubt and certainty, and ignorance and awareness.

Coming to the United States was a wonderful opportunity for us to take advantage of what it had to offer— knowledge, technology, and scientific advances—for the purpose of gaining experience and applying it in our own country. It is eye-opening to see Iran from a different perspective—outside of its borders—removed, so that we can learn from our past, and reflect on the future, and create lovely moments in our present. This is what migration is all about. It is good for those people who learn from their past, plan out their future, and live in the moment.

LEARNING BY EXAMPLE

The jumbo jet carrying four hundred passengers—in all its strength and glory a testament to human achievement and the power of thought—gently landed on the runway at Los Angeles International Airport. The fact that we are able to use science and technology to defy the laws of gravity, taking a plane from one corner of the world to another and flawlessly land it on the ground, is a shining example of humanity's ability to bring ideas to life.

A person who adopts the Technology of Thought always selects a role model to emulate on the journey to greatness, a leader who can quickly and easily take him or her to the land of success. This theme permeates Persian literature: the stories of followers and their leaders.

When we arrived at the Los Angeles airport, my friend was waiting for us with his wife and child. He had already gone through this world of transformation and had experienced

Tap into Your Thoughts

A self-aware person transformed by the Technology of Thought never uses trial and error to create new achievements and never allows poor planning to cause a mistake, a mistake leading to time and money wasted. People who live without role models do not gain from the experiences of others, making bad decisions, while on the other end of the spectrum are people who always use the wisdom and experiences of role models in their quest for success.

Before making a decision, these people find someone who has already successfully accomplished the task and consult him or her. Learning from the examples of others is the shortest path to achieving their own goals successfully. In the Technology of Thought, this phenomenon is known as modeling, or following by example.

thinking and creating. So by sharing his experiences of starting a new life in a foreign land, he would be a model for us to follow.

Perhaps, as I search the world over, what I'm looking for is right in front of me. Islam and the teachings of the prophets and great leaders introduce a phenomenon called "religion," which means "a model for living": how we should

live and achieve happiness, how we should think and create, and how thoughts and ideas are tools for excelling.
The Technology of Thought reveals the secret of human
power.

In any case, collecting these reflections and giving
them a systematic feel is an innovative task performed by
students of self-development the world over. Without sell-
ing ourselves short, we are to travel around the world and
use the advances of other nations and peoples of the world
to create a more beautiful world and a more productive
future for ourselves.

At the airport, greeted by our friends, we began the
dawn of a new life—twelve years of research, education,
and teaching at American universities.

A FOREIGNER IN AMERICA

Although my main goal for coming to the United States
was to continue my education and familiarize myself with
the methods of managing industry there, I still was curi-
ous about the principles of the human thought system.
I wanted to learn more from those who studied self-
development; I wanted to learn how to access the full
potential of human power.

My formal education in Iran consisted of a bachelor's
degree in mechanical engineering from the Sharif University of Technology. I always hoped to pursue a master's

degree and Ph.D. in industrial engineering, and it didn't take long before continuing my education in the field of industrial and systems engineering.

Any topic related to science interested me, and I wanted to find out how I could apply whatever I learned to Iran and how to manage our own industry. I always saw myself as a traveler, an ambassador who comes with a mission on behalf of another country: to absorb all of the positive aspects of scientific and technological advances from a developed country and utilize that knowledge for the benefit of my own country.

After some time, I successfully completed my master's degree and continued on with my Ph.D. in industrial and systems engineering. I also began to teach different courses in industrial engineering at U.S. universities, including the University of Southern California (USC). Before I knew it, I was able to teach at other schools and to have wonderful teaching experiences and sufficient remuneration to allow me to live well. In addition to these endless blessings, another beautiful moment occurred in my life—the birth of my son. He was born at the USC hospital in L.A. We named him Mahdi and hoped that one day he would make valuable contributions to our home-land. Now, not only can he speak English fluently, he is also fluent in Persian.

Being in a foreign land reminded me of a distant memory. When I was a high school student, one day a student about my age came from England to Iran to see Alavi High School. He was sitting in the office of Mr. Alameh, the school's founder, and everyone talked about the boy, saying that he had come from a foreign land and that he spoke fluent English. This became a dream of mine, to one day have a child who, like this boy, could speak perfect English in addition to speaking Persian—one who could become a spiritual speaker in foreign countries. Ask and you shall receive. Indeed, every thought is like a seed that is planted in one's mind and which produces its fruit in the land of life. This is especially true when the thought is created amid a world of hope, conviction, and emotion.

DEVELOPING THE IDEA OF THE TECHNOLOGY OF THOUGHT

The concepts and principles of the Technology of Thought developed over the several years I was in America. Though the main purpose in coming to the United States was to make my long-standing dreams of continuing my education come true, learning and applying the concepts of self-development to my own life was my secondary goal, one I fervently pursued.

Introspective thoughts, reflections, and discussions evolved through many gatherings at congregations, company meetings, and even political, cultural, educational, and economic conventions. At these gatherings, there was always a buzz and excitement championing the ideal that people can choose to live differently. People spoke about planning and managing a new life for those who want to live well and accomplish wonderful things. However, in a materialistic world, the first concerns people had were about money and comfort. The American dream consisted of having a beautiful car, a nice home, an attractive partner, a high level of education—all of the general luxuries associated with wealth and success.

Andrew Carnegie came from humble beginnings to become the most successful man in the American steel industry, the owner of the largest steel company at the time. He told people that man is the creator of his own destiny. He is the foundation of these kinds of discussions about human power. Carnegie had a student by the name of Napoleon Hill, who learned from his mentor's example and achieved a world of success. Hill interviewed hundreds of successful Americans, trying to understand the keys and secrets to their success. He gathered the results of his research and disseminated his wisdom through several popular books. For years, these books were bestsellers in the United States and around the world. I studied different self-help books each day, spending time at libraries in Los Angeles and New York. I was hungry for any material, book, or article that explored human power, the power of thought as well as any issues related to human development.

Tap into Your Thoughts

How can you live differently? How can you plan and manage your life? What is the mystery behind human creation? What is your place in the universe? How can you think and achieve any goal? How can you change the course of destinies?

I pursued discussions on self-development everywhere, doing my own research while attending conferences key-noted by experts in this field. The information I gleaned was put into action in my own life. I then began my mission to share my wonderful findings with others, culminating in what you'll find in the chapters ahead—the principles of the Technology of Thought.

Today, after twelve years of teaching; researching; gathering scientific, cultural, and social experience; and traveling to more than fifty countries, including the United States and Canada and countries in Asia, Europe, and Africa, I have begun my greatest and most productive mission: to let Iran and the world know that "You can choose to live differently."

During these twelve years, I traveled to Iran frequently and was more or less aware of the people's situation. I knew of the political, economic, military, and cultural conditions under which they lived. The nation of Iran had gone through an Islamic revolution and eight years of an imposed war. Economic sanctions, foreign hostility, imperialistic pressure to demolish the new government of the Islamic Republic of Iran, political divisions, and internal disputes were all threatening to innocent people who simply wanted a better life.

Eight years of war weakened the economy and took an enormous toll on the people, most significantly in terms of the lives that were lost. Countless young soldiers died, while many others were left disabled. We needed a transformation to leave behind a turbulent identity and find the motivation to design a future and rebuild a new country in the twenty-first century.

REDEFINING OUR BELIEFS

We must redefine our beliefs and current attitude about the life we live. We must instill positive qualities and change the way we think and embrace a renewed spirit. We must give the word *life* a whole new definition. We must create in people a world of hope and happiness.

On that beautiful Sunday morning, while sitting next to the window on the twenty-first floor of a fifty-story building in New York, my eyes fell upon some sailboats in the water passing near our apartment complex. As I sat there gazing at them, my thoughts drifted to the people in Iran. I thought to myself, "What kind of life do they have at this moment? What type of encouragement and hope are they living with?"

I suddenly exclaimed, "Alireza! Where are you now? What kind of mission and responsibility do you have today? Your mission is no longer to stay in the United States, but rather, with a responsibility similar to that of an ambassador, you must return to your homeland and with the help of other teachers and society's patrons, tell all of the Alirezas and Fatemehs of Iran that indeed, they *can* choose to live differently."

Today my mission, as well as yours, is to create a new world. A world with millions of people who are at peace, in love, respected, filled with self-confidence and self-esteem, living in a state of self-awareness and certainty, their hearts filled with love and hope toward a productive and beautiful tomorrow.

No matter where we are in life and how happy we are, there are always greater successes and joys that we can achieve, and by using the Technology of Thought, we can turn every opportunity into a means of prosperity.

We have no right to ruin our lives. We have no right to live in failure, regret, anxiety, and unhappiness. We must not live in defeat and hopelessness. When faced with life's

Tap into Your Thoughts

Today people need this divine message in order to realize that they have the ability to choose to live differently. Today, people, especially young people, have everything except "belief" in themselves. We must change our belief so that we have faith in our potential and create thoughts anew. We must give hope and encouragement to people who don't think that they can change their lives.

issues and problems, we must not see ourselves as weak, and we must not go through life without purpose and without goals.

We have no right to live in discontentment. We have the responsibility to live in a world created by our positive thoughts. We came into this world to enjoy every single moment, living beautifully in a world of endless blessings.

We must understand that we are living in a gold mine of blessings. We can either remain unsatisfied in this mine, or live in the wealth of this treasure. The most crucial advice I can give you is to discover the gold around you, and with your thoughts, extract these nuggets of wealth. With open eyes, let us see all the splendors of the world in a whole new light, allowing us to think differently and ultimately live differently. And with this new mission, let's turn hate into love, animosity into affection, despair into hope, enmity into friendship, ugliness into beauty, weariness into bliss, weakness into strength, failure into success, inability into ability, war and hostility into peace and camaraderie, exhaustion and fatigue into energy and effort, and turn life into a process of thinking and creating.

In the next chapter, you will find out how the Technology of Thought can lead to the path of success, discovering new tips along the way. And by applying these principles to your thought-generating factory—your mind—you will create invigorating and blissful thoughts, allowing you to achieve the pinnacle of success in your own world.

This book will change your outlook on life and will instill in you wonderful new principles and beliefs about life. *Think Yourself Successful* will transform you into a person who truly enjoys every moment of life.

The word *life* is truly the most meaningful word in existence. Life is the best gift given to us. I hope that this book will help you create a whole new, beautiful you and make you believe that "Yes, it is possible to live differently."

2

THE TECHNOLOGY
OF THOUGHT

*C*enturies have passed, and now humans have begun
to embark on the third millennium, creating a new world
for themselves. History has witnessed all of mankind's great
advancements in science and technology, giving way to
today's amazing accomplishments. Today, we have made
vast progress in industry, agriculture, and communications,
nowhere more so than with computers and satellites.

Computers have rapidly taken over jobs once performed by people, seemingly making life easier. These
machines have a hand in all aspects of people's lives and
are responsible for managing many of their activities. They
are so ubiquitous that if one day computers decided to go
on strike, turning against us, life on earth would become

unimaginably difficult and all administrative systems would come to a catastrophic halt. It is as if, without computers, our lives would come to an end; computers control airplanes, command space shuttles, and drive robots in factories to perform tasks such as building automobiles, without all that much human intervention.

For many years, I pondered a fundamental question: "If we are capable of and have been able to powerfully master all areas of science and technology, programming computers to do almost anything, even change the world that surrounds us, why haven't we done anything for our intellect?"

At the dawn of the new century, we experience various mental, spiritual, and emotional problems, which lead to unsatisfied and unhappy lives. With all of our scientific and technological advancements, why do people still see themselves as powerless? Unhappy, lacking self-confidence and fulfillment, we feel restless and insecure. As time goes by, we feel more and more empty inside.

The rate of divorces, untimely deaths, mental and emotional illnesses, and other social problems have forced us to think about why we live this way, despite the endless discoveries, inventions, and innovations of our time.

I pondered this and thought to myself, "If we are able to control technology so effectively, isn't it possible for us to program our *internal computer* and become a *whole new person*? And in doing so, end all our mental and emotional problems and acquire all the characteristics of an ideal person?"

An amazing "internal computer" exists within us that is in charge of our entire destiny and controls each and every aspect of our existence. It shapes our emotions, beliefs, and self-confidence, our whole identity. If we were able to communicate with this internal computer, understand how it works and program it, we could become a "whole new person"—able to overcome all the obstacles of life, experience transformation and rebirth, and live the best life possible. As a person who has found spirituality, I live in complete health, serenity, and beauty, enjoying every moment of life.

"THOUGHTWARE"

With the Technology of Thought, you can begin a new chapter in your life on the cusp of the twenty-first century. Living by these principles will help you conquer any challenge before you. In the new age, after having gone through an era of "hardware" and "software," we have come to the era of "thoughtware."

The subconscious mind is an amazing part of our humanity that manages and controls our entire being. It shapes behavior, identity, and beliefs. It allows us to form a relationship with other people to fulfill our goals and dreams. In other words, the subconscious mind allows us

Tap into Your Thoughts

The secret to this new technology is the recognition that within us is a magnificent "computer," the subconscious mind. If we program this internal computer the right way, we can change our entire existence.

to use extraordinary powers and create whatever we desire. Although the exact scope and abilities of the subconscious mind have not yet been discovered, I realized that by harnessing this unique internal computer, we can create an amazing life and achieve true happiness.

I named this new perspective on how we create our own successes the Technology of Thought because, for us, everything begins with a thought, the primary signal that goes into our subconscious minds (our internal computer). Our thoughts are what guides and commands our subconscious mind.

TRANSFORMING YOUR SET OF BELIEFS IS THE FIRST STEP TOWARD SUCCESS

Using the Technology of Thought can bring an end to repeating past failures. By transforming from within, you can change your thoughts and set of beliefs to acquire a new identity, ultimately achieving a new world of self-confidence, health, happiness, and peace. This is how you lay the groundwork for a new life—how you think and, by thinking, create anything you desire. You can build strong relationships with people and become a powerhouse of success in all aspects of your life.

Again, everything begins with a thought. A thought is the first step toward any accomplishment. The Technology of Thought utilizes this concept in a systematic, fundamental way. It programs us to automatically think beautifully and creatively.

If we enthusiastically think about knowledge, wealth, health, peace, and spirituality, we will become knowledgeable, wealthy, healthy, and peaceful and become successful in this world as well as the hereafter. This success will come to those who are able to think this way.

The reason why so many people find it difficult to *think and create* is because in principle, the phenomenon of thought is not an independent component within us by which we can, at any moment, create thoughts that are positive, creative, goal-oriented, constructive, inspiring, and productive. Rather, thought is generated from a person's belief system. Therefore, we must first change our set of beliefs before we can change the quality of our thoughts.

Wealthy people have grand and wealth-generating beliefs. With a strong sense of self-confidence they pursue wealth, and—with their positive beliefs—they attain that which they desire. Students who get accepted into great schools believe strongly in themselves; the thoughts generated from their belief drive them to constantly work hard and take positive steps forward, resulting in their acceptance. People who win competitions first see themselves as winners in their mind's eye—and so they win. The law of life is the law of beliefs.

The success of a society is measured by the collective beliefs of its people. If one would like to know where a nation stands in terms of cultural, political, economic, social, and military success at any point in time, it would make sense to poll the beliefs of its people. It is these beliefs and the collection of thoughts stemming from them that form a nation.

Shaping Our Beliefs

Considering the importance of beliefs for our future successes, let us define what a "belief" is and how it is formed during a lifetime.

From the moment people are born, a system begins to take shape inside them—their "belief system." This means that all the information that is gathered though their five senses and every thought that goes though their head is processed by their subconscious and turned into a belief. For example, seeing a red rose, which is a symbol of love, beauty, and nature, becomes a signal that enters the subconscious mind through the eyes and after processing, subconsciously builds a portion of one's belief system, or at the very least affects one's belief system. As a result, when you see a beautiful red rose, you come to believe that "life is beautiful," which is a lovely belief that the subconscious mind creates inside of you. On the other hand, if instead of a beautiful flower you were to see a rotting fruit, the sight would instantly be processed by your subconscious mind to generate a belief within you that "life is ugly and unpleasant." So whereas one signal gives rise to positive thoughts, another brings forth negative ones.

All of the elements of your environment, including media such as the Internet, radio, and television, and especially the people you're around—your mother, father, teachers, friends, and other family members—are all architects building, shaping, and structuring your belief system. Let's say that during your childhood, your math teacher praises you in front of the class for correctly solving a problem. You will begin to believe in your mathematical abilities, and when you come across a math problem, you'll solve it. Why? Because your abilities are determined by your beliefs. In other words, this kind of belief creates a powerful notion inside you, which guides you toward solving the problem. This is the relationship between belief and notion.

If, for example, your ninth-grade chemistry teacher constantly criticized you, saying that you would never be successful at chemistry, chastising you in front of the class, your belief in your ability to excel at chemistry would be shattered. This weakened belief in your abilities would create a notion of failure inside you that would actually cause you to fail.

Beliefs even play an important role in building one's morale. A strong belief in yourself builds confidence, and a weak belief creates uncertainty for achieving success.

What you believe in is what you create. Your achievements in life are built by your beliefs. As it is written in the Quran, "For man, everything is achieved through effort."[1] This, here, is where the role of the subconscious, which is responsible for building a person's beliefs, becomes clear, and the Technology of Thought validates and emphasizes this vital role.

TWO INGREDIENTS OF THOUGHT: BELIEFS AND MORALE

Another important factor that plays an essential role in the quality of our thoughts is our morale. Good morale creates positive, hopeful, and creative thoughts. On the other hand, a withering, depressed, and dejected morale creates negative, destructive, and toxic thoughts.

In addition to beliefs, morale is also a necessary ingredient in the thought process; both must be present and working together to create a thought. Let's imagine that your thoughts are a bird flying with two wings. One wing is powered by your collective belief system, which has been shaped from your birth up until now. The other wing is your morale and the quality of your feelings, which determines where your bird (your thought) will fly and on which branch it will perch after soaring through the sky of your life. The bird that is tired, possessing a discouraged morale and, at the same time, with no positive and character-forming beliefs, always flies with two broken wings; it perches on ruins and broken walls, taking the owner of those thoughts to the brink of destruction.

On the other hand, the bird with high morale, one that possesses wonderful beliefs, always flies with two powerful wings. And like an eagle, it soars to the very peak of a successful life.

You may now be asking yourself, "What is the mechanism inside us that creates these two wings? What phenomenon creates belief and morale inside us?" It is essentially our subconscious mind that generates our belief and morale.

Once you become aware of your subconscious mind and take hold of its powerful reins, you too can always create the best beliefs and the most uplifted morale within you. You can equip your bird of thought with two strong wings and by using them, build and enjoy the best life possible. In the next chapter, we will take a closer look at our unique "internal computer"—our subconscious mind.

3

REPROGRAM YOUR
SUBCONSCIOUS MIND

*I*n the previous chapters, we discovered that everything begins with a thought and that thought is where transformation begins. We *are* what we believe. If people are after success, happiness, and joy in their life, they must know that they can achieve great things and embrace true happiness only by thinking the right, positive, creative, and goal-oriented thoughts.

The difference between individuals is the difference in their belief systems. In fact, the success, happiness, and wealth of each country are determined by the collective beliefs of its people. Our beliefs are constructed by our subconscious mind, and the subconscious mind is like a computer whose input is the information it receives through the five senses, as well as any strand of thought.

It processes the input to create our belief system. If people want to change their thoughts and way of thinking, they must create change in their belief system.

You can change your belief system by sending appropriate signals to your subconscious mind (internal computer). In the next section, I will show you how we can reprogram our subconscious mind for success.

YOUR SUBCONSCIOUS MIND IS AN INTERNAL COMPUTER

Our minds consist of two components: the conscious mind and the subconscious mind. The *conscious mind* takes on the commanding role for our existence and is, in fact, that part of ourselves we refer to as "me." When you consciously make a decision to do something and then carry it out, it is your conscious mind at work. It gives orders, makes judgments, performs analysis and evaluations, and manages your daily activities. The subconscious mind awaits orders from our conscious mind and accomplishes its tasks under its guidance and commands.

The *subconscious mind* is just like a computer that manages and controls our beliefs, characteristics, self-confidence, and identity—it also continuously forms our morale. The subconscious mind at each moment can develop a connection with the subconscious minds of other individuals. Your subconscious mind can create an unconscious communication between you and others (telepathy). In fact, the way I describe telepathy is basically as "bio-computers" communicating with each other. This communication is done in the absence of the conscious mind. Thoughts and feelings are relayed to someone unconsciously. By forming a connection with the universe, the subconscious mind can create a bond between yourself and all of existence, allowing you to realize your supernatural powers. The Quran says, "We brought all that is in the universe under your command."[1]

The power of communication with everything in the universe is called "the Law of Attraction." The subconscious mind receives every single thought as a signal, processes it, and relays it to the universe. The universe responds to this thought and, depending on its nature (positive or negative), produces an appropriate outcome. As Joseph Murphy puts it, "You lose what you condemn, and you attract what you love."[2] By sending negative signals to the universe, you push things away. On the other hand, by communicating positive thoughts, you attract them.

How the Subconscious Mind Works

The subconscious mind, like any other computer, has a series of inputs and outputs and performs a series of processes. The inputs to the subconscious mind consist of information gathered through the five senses as well as any train of thought that goes through one's head. The aggregate of these six input channels constantly feeds the subconscious mind.

This means every piece of information that is received through the five senses as well as any train of thought, in addition to entering the conscious mind, also enters the subconscious mind. After registering and storing this information as separate files, each with a unique identifier, the subconscious mind "computer" processes the information. The result of this processing is the formation of a belief in one's belief system and the building of a particular type of mentality, feeling, or precept, as well as an external effect in the outside world.

Recall our example from Chapter 2 of the beautiful red rose, a symbol of love. When you encounter such a rose, in addition to affecting your conscious mind, this sight (signal) also enters your subconscious mind and after some processing, creates a good feeling within you, producing a wonderful belief: "life is beautiful." When you start to believe that life is truly beautiful, you gain a positive and cheerful mood, and such a belief will inspire hope and action within you and create positive and constructive thoughts in your mind. These positive thoughts will motivate and encourage you toward productive work. They will bring about the achievements you desire. What you think about, you bring about.

On the other hand, if instead of seeing something beautiful like a rose, you run into an extremely rude person, this experience will also be stored in your subconscious mind, but it will create an unpleasant association, forming a negative belief. You will be left thinking, "Why are people so rude?" All information that you acquire throughout the day with your five senses, everything you see, hear, taste, smell, and feel—and every single thought you have at every moment—have their own unique effect on your subconscious mind. These signals are influential in building your belief system as well as your mood, perspective, and state of mind.

Unlocking the Power of Your Subconscious Mind

Once we unlock the power of our subconscious mind, we become capable of using our metaphysical abilities. An example of this can be seen in a sacred account narrated by Imam[3] Ali[4] from the words of the Prophet Muhammad (peace be upon him), wherein God says to him, "Oh my creation, obey me so that I might make you like me, and as I create anything I command, you too will be able to create anything you command." Thus, in addition to our physical and natural powers, another power is envisioned for us, and that is our metaphysical power, one that, according to the Law of Attraction, can bring forth endless possibilities.

Whenever the subconscious mind receives a command from the conscious mind, it has the ability to connect to an extraordinary source of information in the universe, "infinite intelligence." All the information in the universe lies in this informational network. Connecting to it is analogous to a computer connecting to the Internet and the World Wide Web. When a computer makes this connection, all of the information that is available on the Internet is made accessible.

Interestingly, many of the world's scholars have acquired, and still acquire, the solutions to their mysteries and scientific equations by connecting to infinite intelligence through their subconscious mind. By connecting to this network, the subconscious mind is able to form a hidden and unconscious bond with everyone else and their subconscious minds (that are connected to this network) and ask for help from them (through their subconscious minds) in solving any problem or achieving any goal. People who use the Technology of Thought achieve their goals and dreams by unlocking the power of the subconscious to create a wonderful life for themselves.

Many scholars, poets, and artists who do remarkable things and give life to extraordinary works of art, in fact, use the Technology of Thought and their subconscious minds to do so. It is the subconscious mind that led Ferdowsi[5] and Shakespeare to create such masterpieces. It is the subconscious mind that empowered Beethoven, a man of impaired hearing, to compose such beautiful symphonies. It is the subconscious mind that made Hafez[6] and Rumi[7] into the erudite poets that they were, so powerful that one can sense God in each word of their poems.

HOW TO PROGRAM YOUR SUBCONSCIOUS MIND

The subconscious mind works like a computer that can be specifically programmed to achieve desired outputs and results. The result of this processing is an output that forms our belief system and identity, affecting our mood and perception of the external world. Considering the fact that its output is directly related to its input signals, to program the subconscious mind to be successful, we must control its inputs. By controlling the inputs or thoughts of the subconscious, we can control our successes and accomplishments. In the pages ahead, I will show how to systematically control and program the subconscious mind through a set of five principles.

1. The Principle of Consciousness, Self-Awareness, and Constant Insight into Oneself

This principle is the most important one in the Technology of Thought. At each moment, every signal that the subconscious receives builds a corresponding belief and disposition. Therefore, we should always be aware of ourselves and the kinds of signals we receive through our five senses and through our thoughts. This ensures that in a constant state of self-awareness, we send the best possible signals to our subconscious mind.

To this end, the subconscious mind of those who gaze upon the reddest of roses, listen to the chanting of inspir-

Tap into Your Thoughts

In order for you, dear reader, to benefit the most from this book and ultimately become a whole new, beautiful person and live the life you truly deserve, I suggest that you, too, believe that along this path you will transform. You are now on a journey to create a future that has no resemblance to your, perhaps unsuccessful, past. You are to become a powerful person who thinks and creates with the best beliefs and happiest disposition.

At this moment, form a pact with yourself and the higher powers that be to become beautifully transformed as you read this book, page by page, and develop into a loving and erudite person. Someone who is peaceful and kind is someone who thinks and sees positively, and someone of a beautiful character. Through this transformation, you will definitely think brilliantly and live exceptionally.

Remember that you design your own destiny. Your life and fate are shaped by your beliefs and thoughts and are ultimately in your own hands.

ing and positive words, breathe in fragrant aromas, feast on delightful gourmet dishes, sense the subtleties in life at each moment, and inside their thought-generating factory produce positive, creative, goal-oriented, morale-boosting, and constructive thoughts receives the most wonderful of signals and creates life beautifully.

With this attitude, continue reading and know that today an immense transformation will occur in your life: you will be guided onto a beautiful path leading to the masterpiece of your life. Filled with love and emotion, excitement and happiness, determination and resolve, and effort and hope, use the principles of the Technology of Thought and see its tremendous effects on your mind, soul, character, and beliefs. And enjoy your new life—you deserve nothing less.

I commend you for finding a new path for your life and making the effort to create a life of beauty in this world as well as the hereafter. Now here are the rest of the principles to program your subconscious mind.

2. The Power of Focus

Whatever you focus on at each moment is reflected onto your thoughts. For example, focusing on a flower creates a cheerful disposition and positive thoughts in your mind, while focusing on an unpleasant image can bring negative and discouraging thoughts to your mind. Focusing on happy memories brings joy to a person, and focusing on negative ones brings pain. What you focus on has a very important effect on the subconscious mind.

You can program your subconscious mind by constantly focusing on positive past memories and imagining great future successes. When we send positive signals to

Tap into Your Thoughts

For a person who constantly focuses on the misery and ugliness of life, life will be miserable; for someone who constantly focuses on hopeful prospects, life will be happy and successful. This is the nature of focus.

our internal computer, we create wonderful beliefs in ourselves, attract the good things in life, and make our lives happy and hopeful.

You should always try to control your focus. Focus on beautiful scenarios: scenarios that emerge in the world around you, even things that are outside of your control; those you see with your feelings; and also those that take shape in your mind and occupy your heart. Inputs to your subconscious mind can have deep and desirable effects in your life. Be mindful of the things that you focus on.

3. The Power of the Question

Every question that you ask yourself creates a specific reflection of your state of mind. For example, merely asking the question "Why is it that I'm so fortunate?" boosts mood and state of mind, conveying that "Indeed, I am fortunate." This sentiment and thought sends a positive signal to the subconscious mind, where the signal is processed and produces a result that can truly be life-changing and can, in fact, elevate one to true happiness and fortune. Depending on the signals it receives, the subconscious mind makes the universe so in tune with us that it fulfills whatever we desire.

The reverse is also true. When a person asks, "Why am I so unfortunate?" merely asking this question immediately gives off a deflated and despondent outlook. This negative signal enters the subconscious mind and gets processed, where it not only creates a mentality that matches the question, it also affects all of creation in such a way that it builds a wall and barrier preventing good fortune from reaching that person.

It's important to recognize the great effect of each question you ask yourself. You must know that the quality of your life is determined by the type of questions you ask yourself.

Now, considering the effect of each question, what have you decided to do about the kinds of questions you ask yourself every day? Will you be mindful and begin asking yourself positive and invigorating questions, or will you pose negative and destructive ones?

4. The Principle of Using Positive Affirmations

Every sentence that you speak, write, or read has a connotation that is a signal to your subconscious. Therefore, always use positive-emphasis (affirmation) sentences that in some way illustrate your good qualities. These connotations create a reality in your world that is proportional

Tap into Your Thoughts

When asking a question, what is the word you use most often? Is it the word *why* or the word *how*? Do you ask, "Why am I in this situation?" or do you say, "How can I improve the current situation and make it more wonderful?" The difference between these two questions is the difference between misery and happiness, poverty and wealth, depression and bliss, and despair and hope. Indeed, this is how the quality of your life is determined by the type of questions you ask yourself.

If you ask, "Why is everything so screwed up?" everything will indeed be screwed up, and if you ask, "How is it that the universe always wants the best of everything for me?" your entire life will be wonderful. This is the nature of questions. Every question is a signal, a command to the subconscious mind. Now tell me from now on, how careful will you be with the kinds of questions you ask yourself? One question can alter the course of a life.

to the connotations. At the same time, the subconscious mind builds the connotations into your belief system and in this way constantly refines your beliefs. Write inspiring sentences and post them all around you—at work and at home. Constantly read them to yourself and firmly take hold of their meaning. Here are some examples of positive affirmations to get you started. Feel free to create many more of your own!

- There is excellence and greatness within me.
- I am brilliant and I use my brilliance to succeed.
- I have great ideas in my head, and I will bring them to fruition.
- Every day, I am healthier and more in shape.
- I am a winner.
- I am truly a unique and special person.
- My world has become so lovely and beautiful.
- As each day passes, I become happier and more blissful.
- I always become successful and victorious in everything I do.
- I am loved in every aspect of my life.
- Wealth and spirituality are always flowing toward me, and I create anything I desire.
- My entire being is filled with energy and joy.
- I always expect good things in my life.
- I am proud of myself.
- Joy, energy, and love emanate from my being and from my face.
- I will live well for the rest of my life.
- The more I give, the more I receive and the more I feel content.
- I will effectively design my life the way I want.

- I am a powerful, creative, and appealing individual.
- I deserve the very best.
- Every second, I thank God for all the blessings and gifts he has bestowed upon me.
- I live in complete serenity, and I am always in a good mood and of cheerful disposition.
- With great power, I have control over all of the things in my life, my thoughts, feelings, and actions, and I manage them with ease.

Aside from positive affirmations, you can also use positive words and expressions such as *serenity, beauty, spirituality, wealth, well-being, a lovely life, great wealth, health, security, happiness, bliss,* and so forth.

All of these words and expressions have a unique and positive effect on the subconscious mind. They can bring about that exact reality in your life and strengthen positive beliefs about your abilities and potential.

5. The Principle of Imagination and Visualization

The subconscious mind, like any other computer, can receive images, and at each moment it can obtain millions of bytes of information in the form of a picture (imagination and visualization), process it, and produce an outcome.

When you create an image in your head, this exact image is imprinted on your mind, and like a series of signals and messages, it has a specific effect on your subconscious.

Tap into Your Thoughts

The wealthiest and most successful people are those who are best able to fantasize positive images in their minds. You, as a "whole new, beautiful person" should always try to have a positive imagination. As a first step, create the splendors of life in your mind and know that what you visualize (imagine) in your head, you are able to create in reality. This is the power of man. When you visualize, you materialize.

The image is processed, and your subconscious mind can bring the impression of the image to life. For example, imagine yourself buying your dream car to take a trip with someone you love. The weather is perfect, you enjoy listening to the music coming from your car radio, and you indulge your eyes by feasting on the view of the landscape. This very image can come to life, exactly as you see it. One day, you will buy that car and you will drive to the exact places you imagined, on the same roads you visualized in your fantasy. Suddenly, as you pass through a turn in the road, you will realize, "I imagined and pictured this exact scene two years ago, at a time when I couldn't have even thought about buying a car. I only wished and hoped that this beautiful day would come and now I'm living my dream." Using imagination and visualization is one of the best ways to program and guide your subconscious mind.

They say that when he was young, Neil Armstrong, the first person to step foot on the moon, looked up at the moon and said, "Wow, this moon is so beautiful. How great it would be for me to go there and see it up close." He held on to this dream—and he made it come true.

The formula for making all of your dreams come true is shown in the following diagram:

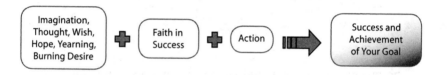

Factors That Help Program Your Subconscious Mind

As we mentioned earlier, a signal coming from any of your five senses is an input that travels to your subconscious mind. That signal is an electronic phenomenon that has two characteristics that define it:

1. **Polarity** that can be either positive or negative, determining the direction of the signal.
2. **Intensity** that determines the power of the signal.

When you think positively and see the beauty in the world, listen to uplifting music, reflect on inspiring affirma-

Tap into Your Thoughts

Turn your fantasy into a thought, your thought into a wish, create hope for your wish, and turn hopefulness into yearning. Bring a world of anticipation to your yearning until it becomes a burning desire, and know that a burning desire along with faith in your dream, along with action, results in success and achieving your goals.

tions, smell a lovely fragrance, or enjoy eating a delicious meal, these positive signals enter your subconscious mind and, in addition to creating a wonderful mental outlook, have a great effect within you and even in the world outside you. The reflection of these beautiful things will come back to you and make your life more and more the life you desire it to be.

The other parameter that distinguishes signals is their intensity, or power. The stronger the intensity of the signals that enter your subconscious, the more of an effect they can have on it. For example, when you ask, "Why am I successful?" this signal has a specific strength, but when you associate the matter with a higher spiritual being and say, "How is it that You have made me so successful?" this sentence transmits a stronger signal to your subconscious mind and will ultimately have a greater effect.

By being spiritual, you create a divine feeling inside you, which allows your subconscious mind to produce wonderful beliefs and helps you achieve your desired goals. As Imam Jafar al-Sadiq[8] has said, "When you call on God for something, you must believe that what you asked for is right behind the door, just waiting for you to take it." In fact, when you ask for something, your faith is a factor that increases the intensity of the signal that enters the subconscious, helping you reach your goal sooner.

Faith, high morale, positive thoughts, confidence in your abilities, trust in your success, great will and determination, a happy and cheerful mentality, and other such states are factors that increase the intensity and power of the signals that enter the subconscious and so quickly take you to the height of success.

In the upcoming chapters, I will show you how you can control and manage your mental outlook to build the foundation for self-confidence. Self-confidence is the first major stop along the path to success.

But, before we end this chapter, I want to give you an example of how you can program and convey positive signals to your subconscious mind. Please read the following section carefully and review it each night before you go to sleep. If you do this every night, your subconscious mind will create wonderful beliefs within you, and as each day passes, you'll reach a greater sense of inner peace and tranquility.

Now with this in mind, imagine me in your presence, speaking to you, now listen calmly . . .

A Look Within

Greetings! I am Dr. Alireza Azmandian, your friend, fellow traveler, and companion.

I wish to speak of love and affection for you, whom I love dearly, and you shall listen to my words in a state of complete peace. Your subconscious mind will hear my words and bring them to life. You will constantly evolve and achieve excellence, inner peace, and inner beauty.

My words will help you use the principles of the Technology of Thought, allowing you to become a sharp, liberated, and free individual who lives wonderfully with complete serenity and self-confidence.

By listening to my words, you will constantly be programmed to have an open and peaceful mind, cheery disposition, fit and attractive figure, and a great feeling toward yourself and others.

Listening to my words will give you tranquility, and you will feel happy and cheerful.

Now, sit peacefully where you are, and in a state of complete focus and serenity, entrust yourself to my words.

The voice you hear is the voice of a friend. The voice of a serene person who cares for you.

Now, I would like for you to feel as though you are at peace. Pay attention to me, focus, and feel calm.

You are now at peace, paying attention, and listening to my voice. Let all of your exhaustion flow out of your body so that you feel more and more tranquil.

Now, take a deep and long breath in, and a long breath out.

Take another deep breath in, and while your whole body is at peace, take another breath out. In this state, slowly close your eyes.

You can easily hear my affectionate voice, and you're paying attention to nothing but my voice, a voice that gives you peace and creates a feeling of love toward your life. A peaceful life awaits you, and you will celebrate it.

Now, take a deep breath in, and as you breathe out, let all your exhaustion and stress flow out of your body, making yourself comfortable. At this moment, now that you are relaxed, look at your toes and loosen them.

This relaxation and release starts in your toes and, like a wave of serenity, flows to your feet and upper body.

Now, loosen up your feet and knees. The wave of relaxation goes up and reaches your back. At this time, your back is completely relaxed. Now loosen up your hands and feel the release and relaxation in your hands.

Now, your neck feels relaxed and the wave of serenity reaches your head.

Your subconscious mind confirms the relaxation of your entire body. It really likes it because it, too, has become relaxed and enjoys having your body at ease. The tranquility engulfs your entire body and even flows through your veins.

Now your head is relaxed. Your mind is relaxed. Your frame of thought is relaxed. In this state, your subconscious mind is relaxed and ready to create wonderful beliefs in you.

At this point, you have a great feeling toward your body. You completely love your body and love yourself.

You have now realized your great character and extraordinary self-worth, and you love your wonderful character.

You have become beautiful and attractive, and each moment and each day, you become more beautiful and more attractive. Every day your body becomes more healthy and fit and you always feel relaxed.

You have found a new path in life—a path of change, growth, progress, success, and happiness.

You have now become acquainted with the Technology of Thought, a system that can make you a whole new person. A person who utilizes all of their blessings and enjoys every second of life. You have now discovered the miracle that is the power of thought. With the power of thought, you can transform your life and acquire wealth. With the power of thought, you can attain health and happiness. You have now realized the amazing power of the subconscious mind.

You now know that your subconscious is the greatest computer in existence. It is an endless treasure within you, at your service. Whatever you command, it executes.

You now command your subconscious mind to change your life and forever keep you in good fortune.

Your subconscious mind will create new beliefs within you and will change your entire life. It will produce wonderful beliefs, goal-driven, positive, and constructive thoughts inside you. Whatever you think of and believe, it will create.

You have begun the Technology of Thought with the Technology of Love. You have tuned in to your spiritual being and you love all the people of the world, and you believe that all people love you as well. You are now serene, free, and full of love, and you have begun a wonderful life.

Now, dear friend, realize how peacefully and beautifully you reflect and pay attention to yourself and your subconscious mind in this lesson, which is your private haven of love.

This lesson is the lesson of secrets. The secrets to your success and the secrets to your love. You are at peace.

You feel great about yourself. You feel as though you are healthy and attractive, with a peaceful and engaging spirit. You realize that in this setting, your body feels calm and you feel serene and powerful.

Now, imagine yourself standing in front of a full-length mirror. What do you see in the mirror?

You see a great person, a creative and successful follower of the Technology of Thought, a transformed and beautiful human being with a wonderful and appealing character.

You look into this mirror, and it reflects the image of your beautiful body. It shows your attractive and lovely clothes, your pleasant and illuminating face, and your kind, loving, and sincere smile. In this mirror, you really see a beautiful person, the same image that other people see when they look at you.

And in this mirror, you truly see the exact image of your subconscious mind.

Now, with this healthy and tranquil body, take a deep breath and feel the tranquility, feel the power, and feel the self-confidence. You truly are a worthy and prosperous person.

You are filled with a feeling of worth and dominance, a feeling of significance, a feeling of being a humble and kind person who is valuable to everyone, and a feeling of being a good believer in the higher powers that be.

Be proud of yourself, because it is with the Technology of Thought that you have chosen to be this way, and you have thought this way, and you are what you think. Therefore, you think wonderfully and optimistically, and you are significant and great.

From this point on, you will live with complete health, well-being, joy, and happiness. You are now a whole new person and have begun a rebirth, a new life. With the Technology of Thought, you have become a true human being and always sense the power of spirituality at your side. Now you are never alone, and other people are all your friends, who enjoy your acquaintance and companionship.

You are a completely well-intentioned and friendly person.

You are successful at everything you do, and for you, every experience is the beginning of a great success. You are a charmer of people and a magnet for wealth and riches. Based on the principle of self-awareness, you always pay attention to yourself and your subconscious mind. You live with prominence, magnificence, and pride. When you look into other people's eyes, you feel as though everyone loves you. With the infinite power of your subconscious mind, you accomplish anything you desire. Each day for you is different from the last, and every day you create a new success and register it in your journal of successes.

Now, open your eyes and take a deep breath and look at the beauty that surrounds you and say, "Thank you, for making me successful, happy, tranquil, and liberated and showing me the best path of life and excellence. I celebrate every day of my beautiful life."

4

MANAGE YOUR
STATE OF MIND

A positive state of mind comes from constructive and morale-boosting signals absorbed from one's environment. Meanwhile, mental and emotional instability and feelings of emptiness, regret, and powerlessness come from destructive signals entering your subconscious mind. Managing your state of mind has an important influence on creating the perfect environment that produces the kind of life you want for yourself.

Today, there are many people who live with depression, stress, and mental and emotional instability. Their lives are filled with so much pain that they seek relief in sleeping pills and anti-anxiety pills, and sometimes even drugs and alcohol, creating the worst kind of life for themselves.

Generally speaking, there are two kinds of people: Type 1 people and Type 2 people. They can be classified based on their mental and emotional characteristics.

Type 1 people are those who generally think positively. They're full of hope and believe that indeed life is beautiful. Their mind is always focused on the splendors of life. They speak positively and optimistically, have smiling faces, and are aware that they are blessed. They think that everything happens in the best possible way for them. They never think about the obstacles or difficulties that they encounter in life. These people usually tell uplifting stories and recall happy memories, which they share with others. They imagine great things for their future. They are self-confident, and they know that their future will definitely be better than their past. They think about their health and well-being. They do not fear the future. These individuals are the followers of the Technology of Thought.

Type 2 people—at the other end of the spectrum— are those who have a pessimistic outlook and other negative characteristics. They lack hope and constantly focus on their hardships. They recall bad memories from their past and visualize negative things for their future. These people's unhappy perspective about their lives is often reflected in their frowning faces.

The important questions to ask yourself are, "How can I become a Type 1 person? How can I create such a transformation in my attitude and outlook on life? How do I manage my disposition so that I'm cheerful, joyful, and happy? How can I create the best things with wonderful thoughts, and transform my life?"

RELATIONSHIP BETWEEN STATE OF MIND, THOUGHT, AND SUCCESS

The most important factor that determines how you feel at each moment is your state of mind. If you have a positive outlook, you think of success, and when you think of success, you achieve wonderful things—and thus become more positive—feeding into a continuous cycle. You produce thoughts of success that guarantee your cheerfulness, bliss, joy, and happiness. It is clear those positive thoughts, stemming from a state of mind that exudes success, will result in amazing achievements.

Someone who has a defeatist and restless mentality thinks negatively, and his or her awful thoughts will have unpleasant consequences. When you are down on yourself, your mind produces negative and destructive thoughts, and those negative thoughts result in negative outcomes like failure, which, in turn, affects your attitude and state of mind—and you are doomed to repeat a cycle that leaves you defeated and powerless.

Considering the strong relationship between state of mind, disposition, and success, you must program yourself to systematically and fundamentally maintain a happy and cheerful mentality. By controlling your state of mind each and every moment of your life, you will live joyfully. You will have conditioned yourself so that negative and destructive thoughts will never enter your mind. Here are some specific techniques so that you can reprogram your state of mind for success.

1. Achieve Tranquility by Feeling That You Are Always in the Presence of God or a Higher Spiritual Being

It's imperative to tune your mind and become aware of your important place in a world that is overseen by a higher spiritual power. If you know that you come from a source of higher spiritual power, you will reach a world of happiness, tranquility, bliss, and hope—and you will understand that you are not alone. To achieve tranquility, we must never forget that we are part of creation on a grander scale.

2. Use the Power of Focus to Control Your State of Mind

I mentioned earlier that we have the ability—the power of focus— to program our subconscious and create within us a more positive disposition and state of mind. If, for a while, you constantly focus your mind on past successes, eventually you will make a habit of always thinking about all the great things that life has to offer. You will essentially transform into an optimistic person, one who basks in inner joy and always feels serene and happy.

Two of the best sources of these kinds of positive scenarios on which to focus are fond old memories and dreams of future success. Therefore, I suggest that you take mental notes of all your life's wonderful past memories and store them in the archives of your mind. Every day, whenever you get the chance, take out one of these past memories and focus on it with the same feeling of enjoyment you had when you first experienced it.

When you are done going through your fond memories, start fantasizing about your dreams, goals, and future success. Create visualizations of a wonderful future and replay them in your head, and soon you will reach a world of pleasure and serenity.

Since each thought and fantasy is a signal to your subconscious mind, and these signals are processed to create a set of beliefs about your abilities, the mechanism of using the power of focus eventually makes you the embodiment of the Technology of Thought—someone who always has a positive outlook, which gives way to great beliefs about his or her potential for success.

When using the power of focus, there is an important difference between thinking about past memories and fantasizing about the future. When you fantasize about the future, you are really hitting two birds with one stone.

Not only are you boosting your morale, but to top it off, whatever you visualize you can make a reality. This is your power. Every phenomenon that you create in your life you first develop in your mind, and whatever develops in the mind can be made into reality.

3. Use the Power of the Question to Control Your State of Mind

Another mechanism through which you can regulate your state of mind to achieve serenity and joy is asking the right questions. I mentioned earlier that the quality of your life is determined by the type of questions you ask yourself. This means that when you ask yourself a positive question such as, "How is it that I am so fortunate and happy?" it becomes a signal that enters your subconscious and creates within you a sense of joy and positive beliefs about yourself.

At the same time, a feature of the subconscious mind is that with every question it receives, your mind immediately searches to find the conditions to bring the meaning of the question to life. Therefore, by using the power of the question, you are actually hitting two birds with one stone. You are both boosting your morale and bringing the meaning of the question to life through your subconscious mind. So it is important for you to constantly ask yourself positive, key questions to shape the kind of life you want.

Tap into Your Thoughts

The power of focus and the power of the question are like two powerful wings that help you acquire a cheerful and positive state of mind, granting you the ability to take flight so that in the sky of your life, you can fly with tranquility and reach the highest peaks of success.

Now that you know how to manage your state of mind and regulate your thoughts, giving way to a more positive outlook on your life, you can begin to create the life that you want. In the next chapter, I will introduce other dimensions of the Technology of Thought and show you how to build the foundation for unstoppable self-confidence.

5

GAIN ULTIMATE
SELF-CONFIDENCE

*G*aining confidence and self-esteem is another stop on your journey to success. Your entire character is shaped by your self-esteem, which is a prerequisite for self-confidence. Self-confidence is the manifestation and expression of self-esteem to the outside world.

Self-esteem is the value and worth you assign to yourself and how much you cherish yourself. Feelings of admiration, greatness, and belief in yourself define your self-esteem. Tell me how you feel about yourself. Do you feel a sense of greatness and importance within you? Your future success both in your life and your career absolutely depend on this feeling.

One of the main factors that affects your level of self-esteem is self-understanding. People who do not have a good understanding of themselves cannot have good self-esteem and therefore don't have self-confidence. Now the question is, "How can we understand ourselves better?"

If for a moment you consider the origins of your creation, you will recognize how special you are as a human being. Any feelings of self-doubt, self-loathing, hopelessness, misfortune, and loneliness are all contrary to the position, status, greatness, and power of human beings. Since you are the highest of all creations, you must not doubt yourself.

Just take a minute to think about all the wonders within you, reflect on your place in the universe, discover your greatness, feel eminent, and realize how much you are loved. As you are the highest of all creations, God wants you to be successful in everything you do, excel, and live beautifully.

Self-confidence is a major first stop along the path of a successful life. It indicates the courage and strength of your internal being. It demonstrates your capability in confronting problems in the arena of life. Self-confidence instills certainty within you. It gives you magnificence. It sets you apart from others. Self-confidence is the prerequisite to beautiful and productive relationships. Those who have great self-confidence and combine it with humility and congeniality create a cheerful, attractive, and adored image. Self-confidence is at the root of humankind's growth and excellence. It is the foundation of one's belief system—for each belief begins with the belief in yourself.

Tap into Your Thoughts

Believe in yourself, because your happiness in this life and the hereafter depends on it. Believe in yourself so that all of creation believes in you. Believe in yourself so that the world and the manifestations of its beauty smile upon you and everything goes as you wish. Believe in yourself so that other people believe in you.

If you want to see how others think and feel about you, just take a look at the kind of feeling and sense of self-worth that you have about yourself; others will feel the same.

Here's an interesting verse from the Quran, wherein the Lord addresses His worthy believers who have passed all of God's tests and are on the path toward the afterlife to finally meet their creator. At the gates of heaven, the Lord gloriously greets them: "Oh content soul! Return to your Lord, as He is pleased with you, and you are pleased with Him. Thus enter among my devotees, enter my paradise."[1]

In this verse, the phrase "content soul" is one worth contemplating. One of the main signs of contentment is self-confidence. Therefore, God describes his successful and happy believers with the term "content soul," which conveys the fact that one's happiness in this world and the hereafter depends upon possessing this attribute.

Those who are self-aware cause their subconscious mind to inevitably develop great self-confidence. Acknowledging yourself sends powerful signals to your subconscious, setting the foundation for truly believing in yourself and your abilities.

Now that we know how self-confidence affects success, let's take a look at specific ways we can create strong confidence within ourselves to succeed in all areas of life. In this chapter you will find a set of principles known as the Thirty Principles of Self-confidence. Implementing these principles in your life will automatically create confidence in yourself.

THE THIRTY PRINCIPLES OF SELF-CONFIDENCE

Write down or type up the following principles and place them where you can see them throughout your environment, because every time you glance at and go over these principles, you send a powerful signal to your subconscious that automatically generates great confidence within you.

Principle 1: Remembering, Trusting, and Relying on a Higher Power

This principle is one of the most important principles to continually create self-confidence. When you feel as though you are alone and have no one to rely on, you instinctively become anxious and depressed, losing your confidence. On the other hand, when you have someone or something to lean on (a higher spiritual being), especially mentally and emotionally, you feel more calm and self-confident. This foundation of support can be drawn from God or another higher being you may believe in.

For those who are able to continually remind themselves they are not alone, a wonderful thought enters their subconscious and acts as a powerful signal that results in amazing self-confidence.

Principle 2: Self-Awareness, Consciousness, and Constant Insight into Yourself

This principle is the most influential one in the Technology of Thought and the acquisition of self-confidence. It's important to be aware that your future has no resemblance to your failed past and that everything in your world has changed for the better—and to continually communicate with your inner self to remind yourself of this. Always remind yourself that you are transformed—a person who has reached a world of tranquility, someone who has developed a divine character and who is committed to designing and managing a beautiful life. By doing this, you build hope, belief, self-confidence, and character.

Some people live in a world of unawareness and ignorance toward themselves. These people are never introspective and don't pay attention to themselves. They do not know who they are, what they are doing, and where they are going. They don't have lifelong plans, goals, dreams, or aspirations. They believe that, "What is going to happen, will happen." These people lack self-confidence. They do not believe in themselves, nor do they value themselves. When faced with life's obstacles and difficulties, they very quickly feel powerless and turn to despair. These are the qualities of people who live in a world of self-ignorance. In the Technology of Thought system, we classify them as Type 2 people.

The exact opposite of this world of ignorance is the beautiful world of those who have been transformed by the Technology of Thought. The world of those who live in complete self-awareness. Such people are always aware of their powerful presence in the universe and in the scheme of life. They constantly ask themselves, "Who am I? Where am I? What am I doing?" They are always evaluating their life and asking themselves, "Am I taking the right path in life? Am I thinking correctly? Am I making the right judgments? Do I pursue any goals in my life? Are my future goals completely clear to me? Am I working hard each day to achieve my goals? Am I a successful individual? Do I believe in my full potential? Do I have a healthy level of self-confidence?" These are Type 1 people, and they are constantly self-aware.

Tap into Your Thoughts

Indeed, you have become a "whole new, beautiful person," and at each moment you convey to your subconscious: "Yes, something wonderful has happened. I am a new person who is in control of my life."

You are magnificent, full of self-confidence and self-esteem. You think beautifully and see things in a positive light. You are healthy, dearly loved, with a bright spirit that inspires cheer, and you possess thousands of other beautiful qualities. This is the very meaning of the principle of self-awareness and constant vision and insight into oneself.

By reading this book, you are going to create a transformation in every area of life. Know that you are a person who is always conscious of the principle of self-awareness. You believe that a miracle has occurred in your world, making you a new person. Everything in your world is different. You are in the process of creating a future that, most likely, has absolutely no similarities to your unpleasant past. You must always tell yourself, *"Farewell, my past. I warmly welcome my beautiful future."* The importance of this principle lies in the fact that you create the transformation within your subconscious. This requires constant self-awareness and insight about yourself.

Principle 3: The Principle of Altering Patterns and Creating Reminders

This principle is what guarantees the follow-through of the second principle of self-confidence. Since we are often forgetful, we don't always pay attention to ourselves or worry enough about building our self-confidence. At first, it may be challenging to continually remind yourself, "Indeed, I am a whole new, successful person." You may forget to feed your subconscious, which is always waiting to receive beautiful and positive signals to create new beliefs within you. This forgetfulness can hinder your transformation.

To prevent this from happening, you must create constant reminders and special signals for yourself. For example, if you have a habit of always wearing your watch on your left hand, remove your watch from your left hand and place it on your right, and as you do so, say to yourself, "I'm a whole new person, one who is constantly aware and will unlock all of my potential to create success in my life." So from now on, whenever you instinctively seek your watch to see what time it is, you won't find it on your left hand but rather on your right, and you will instantly think of the mantra: "I'm a whole new person, one who is con-

Tap into Your Thoughts

When altering your habits to associate new actions with the principles of the Technology of Thought, you create these positive beliefs: I am a person of great potential, with a world of self-confidence and self-belief; a person with thousands of creative and morale-boosting thoughts; a person for whom each day is better than the last; one who travels on the path of excellence; one who thinks and creates; a person who climbs life's ladder of success every day.

stantly aware and will unlock all of my potential to create success in my life." This action is called altering patterns and forming reminders.

Now execute this principle in every aspect of your life. Change all of your behavioral habits in an improved way to form reminders for yourself that are like guideposts to correct your path in life. By doing this, you constantly send your subconscious mind positive signals to build up your beautiful beliefs.

Today is the day to alter the decor of your home. Create signs reminding you that "Yes, there's a special something going on in my world. I have become a whole new,

Tap into Your Thoughts

Using the principles of the Technology of Thought in your everyday life is simple, but its results are amazing. It changes you; it transforms you. It gives you a charismatic character and raises you to the level of a divine person, to a world of tranquility and happiness, filled with self-confidence. It takes you from yourself to a higher spiritual power and makes achieving greatness possible.

I congratulate you on discovering the beautiful path of life. You are pure and loving, kind and sincere, decisive and firm, confident and unwavering, and optimistic and self-assured—you are someone with a great future!

beautiful person." For example, if you have a picture on your wall at home, just hang it crookedly for a change, so that each time you look at the crooked picture and think, "Why is this picture crooked?" you answer, "Because *I* have become 'straight,' thereby allowing me to see the crookedness of other things. I have become a whole new, beautiful person." Such changes are signals to the subconscious to establish great beliefs in you that will develop your self-confidence. This is a unique technique for programming the subconscious mind. As another example, change your daily route and take another path for a while. Why? Because you have become a whole new and successful person.

Principle 4: The Principle of Self-Understanding ("Who Am I?")

As a successful student of the Technology of Thought and based on the principle of self-awareness, you continually pay attention to yourself and your subconscious. You evaluate and control your presence in the universe. Therefore, you always ask yourself, "Who am I?"

To answer this question not only forces your conscious mind to reflect, evaluate, and improve your character, it also acts as an important input signal to your subconscious mind that prompts an evaluation of your character, so that new beliefs take shape in your belief system. By constantly asking yourself "Who am I?" you will be better able to discover your inner self and allow your ideal character to take shape.

For example, when you ask yourself and your subconscious "Who am I?" to answer this question your subconscious mind searches your "character files" and creates a belief within you that, for instance, you are a brave, beautiful, capable, kind, loving, and tranquil individual. Thus,

Tap into Your Thoughts

Believe in yourself so that you see yourself as beautiful. Know that others see in you that which you see in yourself. The principle of self-worth is an important principle of self-confidence. Feel it with every molecule of your entire being.

the process of answering this simple question alone forms self-confidence in you.

Principle 5: The Principle of Sensing Your Self-Worth, Self-Greatness, and Character

As a student of the Technology of Thought, you must constantly sense yourself. Sense your worth, beauty, charismatic character, and inner greatness.

Continuous insight into yourself requires seeing a beautiful image of yourself in the mirror of your heart and mind, an image that you genuinely believe in. Emoting this feeling is a powerful signal to your subconscious mind that brilliantly lifts your beliefs and takes you to a world of self-confidence. Essentially, any attention you pay yourself in a positive light forms a constructive signal in the depths of your subconscious, leading to a brilliant outcome. People who are ignorant of themselves forget their character and don't provide their subconscious mind with the input it needs to enhance their belief system and hence their self-esteem and self-confidence.

Those who live in self-awareness always believe in their inner beauty, and therefore, they strengthen their character. Always sense your self-worth and feel as though you are great. Believe me, you are.

Principle 6: The Principle of Self-Belief and Alignment Alongside a Higher Spiritual Being

As a person transformed by the Technology of Thought, you have redefined yourself. You believe that a higher spiritual power is the axis of the entire world and all of creation. But there is also a secondary axis, a representative on earth—you. In its movement, all of creation is aware of this axis and in one way or another acts under its command and control.

Having such an eminent role makes you feel that in the world of existence your essence, as a representative of a higher power, is what matters. It shines so magnificently— and the entire universe is at your command.

This concept is expressed in the Quran in the following way: "We brought all that is in the universe under your command." In a sacred narrative, God says, "I created all that is in the universe for you and I created you for me." This concept is a beautiful belief that everything was created because of you, under your command.

Being aware of this concept allows us to believe in our-selves. In addition to never comparing ourselves to other phenomena in the world, we also see ourselves as an axis on which other things and creatures rotate. This gives us great self-confidence and creates a wondrous character in the framework of our existence.

Principle 7: The Principle of Strength Versus Weakness

In your own world, what kind of reaction do you nor-mally show when faced with different issues and chal-lenges? Do you feel powerful or weak? People who have self-confidence do not see themselves as bound to life's obstacles and events. Rather, they always feel powerful and believe that they will overcome their obstacles with ease.

Surely, as a student of the Technology of Thought, you must always emit a sense of power, not weakness. Feeling powerful or weak does not necessarily have to do with your physical condition or other strengths, such as mon-etary, scientific, or artistic abilities. A feeling of power or weakness is connected to your spiritual state; it is a feeling that depends on a person's character and self-confidence. People who rely on God or another spiritual being feel powerful because they know that they will always have a protector and defender. This sense of spiritual power pro-motes self-confidence.

Tap into Your Thoughts

Indeed! You are a Type I person; you fully believe in yourself. In all matters of life, you evaluate yourself and make decisive choices. You believe that *your* decision is important, *your* opinion is important.

Whatever *you* prefer and choose is important. You never wait for others. You resolve to do something, make decisions, and execute them with success and unwavering determination. This is the nature of a person who lives in a world of certainty.

The world of certainty is the world of beliefs, resolutions, decisions, and actions. Such a world is the world of success—a world of effort and tranquility. This is the world of joy and happiness; this beautiful world is *yours*.

Principle 8: The Principle of Certainty Versus Doubt

As we mentioned in previous discussions, people fall into one of two groups: Type 1 people or Type 2 people. Type 2 people live in uncertainty. They are the kind of people who don't believe in themselves, who always consider others to be more important, and feel insecure in all areas of their lives. Type 2 people always depend on others and wait for others to act before making decisions. These people live in a world of doubt, instability, and identity crisis. They are always spiritually exhausted and depressed. Additionally, their actions in life are doomed to fail because they are always in a world of "in-betweens," waiting for others to make decisions for them. A world of uncertainty exists for those who lack self-confidence, and doubt is a major destroyer of self-confidence and self-esteem.

Type 1 people, on the other hand, are the exact opposite: they are individuals who live in a world of belief and self-confidence, a world of certainty, a world of beauty and character.

It's worth mentioning that although a person like yourself lives in a world of certainty and belief, that does not mean you never consult anyone else. Just as in the Quran the Benevolent Lord advises his prophet to "consult in matters,"[2] we should always consult with experienced and knowledgeable people. You can still practice decisiveness when combining knowledge, experience, and consultation.

Principle 9: The Principle of Leadership and Management

People who have great self-confidence always utilize the qualities of leadership when they manage their affairs. It is interesting to note what generally happens when a group of children in a neighborhood decide to play together and need to divide themselves into teams. Prior to picking teams one child might yell out, "Who's with me?" meaning "Who will join me and play on my team?" At the same time another child, with a timid voice and a sense of self-deprecation, might say, "Who am I with?" meaning, "Who will accept me on his team?" This simple scenario reveals two types of personalities. One personality type is that of a child who lacks the ability to lead and manage a group of people. The other is that of a child who feels like a leader. People who have great self-confidence have a strong sense of leadership.

A person like you, who by reading this book has become a successful student of the Technology of Thought, should always sense this feeling of leadership. In social activities, you should take initiative and guide and direct others and have others follow you. As a result, your subconscious mind, which oversees your actions and activities, will feel you are a leader and that you are capable of managing. Consequently, it will enhance your beliefs about yourself and improve your self-confidence.

Principle 10: The Principle of Accepting Responsibility

People who have a healthy amount of self-confidence are people who accept responsibility. So if you want to build self-confidence, practice taking on responsibilities. Begin by accepting fairly simple ones. For instance, when you go on a picnic with a group of your friends or family, tell them, "I will take on the responsibility of bringing the food!" The act of saying this, alone, is a very powerful signal to your subconscious that causes it to increase self-confidence. Accept responsibility in different areas of your life to strengthen your self-confidence.

Feel responsible when it comes to other people's needs as well. One of the character traits of a whole new, successful person is feeling responsibility toward others and their problems, and rushing to their assistance as much as possible.

Principle 11: The Principle of Cleanliness and Physical Appearance

A person's physical appearance and cleanliness have a direct relationship to his or her self-confidence. A person who wears neat, tidy, and clean clothes has better self-confidence than someone who appears untidy.

Those transformed by the Technology of Thought are individuals who constantly evaluate and improve their physical appearance. The subject of cleanliness and hygiene can also be a sign of faith, an expression of the truth that a faithful believer who has great self-confidence has cleanliness and tidiness as character traits. Therefore, pay special attention to your physical appearance and hygeine, and know that your outer beauty adorns your beliefs.

Principle 12: The Principle of Speaking Highly of Yourself and Others

The subconscious mind is responsible for receiving input signals from the five senses and from any train of thought, processing them, and building beliefs. Therefore any praise that a person hears from others, especially when it is sincere, gets processed in the subconscious and builds stronger self-confidence.

Similarly, a healthy amount of self-recognition causes the subconscious mind to listen to this praise and creates confidence within the individual. Although it is considered impolite for a person to boast about himself, nevertheless, when you tell yourself that you are a beautiful human being or that you are a powerful person, this boosts your self-confidence through your subconscious mind. Now, let us see how a person can be made the object of other people's praise, compliments, and commendations.

Every person innately likes to be praised, complimented, and spoken highly of by others. When someone recognizes you by saying something like "How articulately you speak!" or "What beautiful handwriting you have!" or "What nice clothes you are wearing!" it makes you happy, and you convey your happiness to the person giving praise. Thus, like a mirror, received praise reflects the positive signal back to the other person. This is why someone being commended usually does not remain silent but rather speaks up and reciprocates by saying, for instance, "Your eyes see beautifully"[3] or "You've dressed quite fine yourself today." This, in fact, is exactly what we strive for—to do something that causes others to sing our praises.

Therefore, be mindful to return praises; wherever appropriate, you should praise and compliment others and commend their good qualities. The principle of speaking highly of others not only increases the self-confidence of both individuals, but also enhances your relationship. One sincere word of praise can open the floodgates of kindness and love, bringing two hearts closer together in friendship.

You, too, should practice the principle of speaking highly of yourself and others and make it one of your own positive characteristics.

Principle 13: The Principle of Encouraging Yourself and Others

Encouragement is one of the factors in increasing self-confidence. When people are encouraged and cheered on, their subconscious creates self-confidence, and they believe in their own abilities even more. Therefore, one way to create self-confidence among others is to appropriately encourage them.

At the same time, positively encouraging yourself is also one of the techniques of the Technology of Thought.

It raises the level of self-belief and self-confidence. Therefore, I suggest that whenever you get the chance, observe your own admirable qualities, behavior, achievements, and successful accomplishments. Give yourself encouragement. Pat yourself on the back and tell yourself, "Nice job."

Principle 14: The Principle of Avoiding Self-Criticism and Criticism of Others

Just as encouragement can be a factor in building self-confidence, taunting and criticizing yourself and others is a factor in demolishing the foundation of self-confidence.

Even if you make a mistake that results in a defeat, failure, or some unpleasant outcome, you must remind yourself that "I gained experience and will do it right next time and be successful." In this way, you will continue building the foundation of self-confidence. Fathers, mothers, teachers, and managers should also follow this principle closely to achieve the greatest results in educational environments. Commend and praise yourself and others, and remember that punishment and taunting for failure has more of a destructive effect than a constructive one.

Principle 15: The Principle of Health and Taking Care of Yourself

A person's health also has a direct relationship to his or her self-confidence. When people see themselves as being physically weak, this unconsciously has a negative effect on their spiritual and emotional abilities.

Healthy people are usually better at securing spiritual wellness. As the popular expression says, "A healthy mind is in a healthy body." For example, people who exercise, and by doing so improve their physical well-being, believe in themselves more.

A healthful, nutritious diet and daily exercise help boost your self-confidence. Therefore, exercise, keep yourself in shape, eat appropriate foods, respect your beautiful body, bask in wellness, and watch the effect it has on your success and fortune.

Principle 16: The Principle of Smiling!

Smiling is a direct and tangible sign of having self-confidence and self-belief. Smiling jump-starts beautiful human connections. People who smile show that they are personable, while individuals who are shy and lack confidence tend to smile less often. People who show a beautiful side of themselves by smiling enjoy improved self-confidence, which in turn causes others to also strongly believe in them.

So turn your frown upsidedown and smile. Showing your smiling face reflects to the whole world your satisfaction with your life's great achievements and creates confidence in yourself.

Principle 17: The Principle of Expressing Love Toward Others and Pointing Out Their Good Qualities

Expressing love toward others increases a person's self-confidence. When you tend to a child and show him or her kindness and affection, in a way, you unconsciously sense your greatness and importance to that child. If you express affection for others, especially your loved ones, this not only boosts your self-confidence but also helps immensely to create connections and relationships, which are the keys to your success in life.

Therefore, as a successful student of the Technology of Thought, show love toward people, and point out their good qualities.

Principle 18: The Principle of Perceiving Others and Yourself with Humility

The way you perceive others has a direct relationship to your self-confidence. People who feel powerless when facing others damage their self-confidence. No matter whom you encounter, even if they are highly ranked or positioned, you should not feel weak. Rank and position are merely agreements that will someday expire.

You who hold the highest position in the universe, you have no reason to feel weak or scared when facing other people. On the contrary, you should know that your eminent position is of a superior standing because of the fact that you are a human being. So even though you show humility toward others, at the same time you are aware that your humility is due to your dignity and greatness. You are like the stalk of a prolific, fruit-bearing tree. You are humble and yet aware of your inner beauty and self-belief.

This kind of outlook is very important in your relationships. As a result, your belief system and self-confidence not only remain unblemished, but also, the foundation of your beliefs each day becomes more and more adorned with divine light.

Principle 19: The Principle of Helping Others and Showing Compassion

Essentially, when you help others and show compassion and the forgiveness in your heart, your subconscious thinks of you as being wealthy because you are giving and great because you are forgiving.

The simple act of giving or forgiving has an extraordinary positive effect on your self-confidence. If you were to give even a small amount of change to someone in need, it will cause your subconscious to consider you rich and create the feeling of a rich person inside you. You will immediately feel good about yourself and feel a boost in self-confidence.

Try it today. Take a look around your home or workplace and see what things you rarely use such as articles of clothing, a dish, or anything that doesn't make much of a difference in your life. Separate these items from your other belongings and put them aside. Tomorrow, give them to someone in need and discover the spiritual satisfaction, the feeling of strength and confidence you gain through your compassionate act.

It might interest you to know that sometimes material things for which we have no use can actually be barriers against the downpour of blessings. So when you remove these barriers by donating them to charity, you make way for additional fortune and blessings. When you clean out your closet of all old and unused clothes and give them away, you'll find that the same closet will become filled with new clothes that you were able to buy because of your improved financial ability, caused by this humanitarian act. This is the gift of charity in return—you will be amazed.

Principle 20: The Principle of Honesty, Truthfulness, and Keeping Your Promises

The subconscious mind is very sensitive to the promises you make and the honesty and truthfulness of your character. When you break a promise or act in a way that contradicts your honesty and truthfulness, it has a negative effect on your self-confidence; it shatters your belief system.

People who have high self-confidence are committed to keeping their word. They see themselves as being so great that they never feel the need to lie or make false promises. They are completely honest, and so are their actions, behaviors, and thoughts. Honest people always hold their heads up high and live tranquilly.

Principle 21: The Principle of Avoiding Transgressions

A person's beautiful character has a direct relationship with his or her actions and behavior. People who have a good character and a healthy dose of self-confidence usually don't show any tendency to purposely commit a wrong. Committing a transgression causes the character of a person to be damaged. For example, being pulled over for running a red light, apologizing to the police officer, one's entire character comes into question, and one's self-confidence suffers a blow.

Your inner being has been transformed with the Technology of Thought. You have a strong belief in yourself and a deep understanding of your remarkable character. You are constantly building the foundation of your beliefs. Even in the middle of the night, when the streets are clear and there is no police officer around, when you arrive at a red light, you stop and wait until the light turns green. You do this not because of the police or others, but simply because of your character. Your subconscious mind has become conditioned to stop at red lights. If you were to just drive on through it, your subconscious would consider your action contrary to your character, and this would damage your self-confidence and hurt your character.

Therefore, know that at each moment, your subconscious mind is building your character and is aware and mindful of all your thoughts and actions. *Take care of your subconscious mind, so that it takes care of your joy, happiness, and health.*

Principle 22: The Principle of Decisiveness and Saying No

Saying no is very hard for many people. When faced with an unreasonable request, only those people who have self-confidence are able to say no.

Maybe it has happened to you many times: you're faced with a request that you do not at all want to grant, but you are unable to say so, and so you reluctantly agree. Do you remember how much grief you were caused or how much of your time was wasted because you couldn't say no?

Practice saying no, so that whenever someone makes an unreasonable request of you, you can politely decline. This will increase your self-confidence. Of course, saying no to others must be done very skillfully and delicately to make sure that their feelings are not hurt (this is a topic we will cover in more detail in the next chapter). Eventually, you will become accustomed to declining requests with kindness and humility. When you politely say no, not only do you put yourself at ease, you also give a boost to your self-confidence.

Principle 23: The Principle of Knowledge and Experience

Knowledge and experience also have a direct relationship to self-confidence. Those who know more have more faith in their abilities, while those who are ignorant have less so. As it is emphasized in the Quran, "Are the knowledgeable and the ignorant equal?"[4] Man's knowledge is the foundation of his beliefs.

Of course, it is not possible for one person to know, or be able to do, everything. The point is that each person should have enough knowledge in his or her field of expertise. For example, the accountant of a firm should keep up with current knowledge on the subject of accounting by reading books, articles, and doing research. Activities that promote your expertise will boost your self-confidence every day. If you attend a meeting with your coworkers, employees, or managers, your knowledge base will allow you to present yourself with confidence.

Principle 24: The Principle of Organization and Work Ethic

Organization is one of the most important factors of success and self-confidence. People who are organized are

Tap into Your Thoughts

You must learn to believe in yourself. Gain experience and knowledge so that you see yourself as capable. At each moment, educate yourself so that you always have a sense of self-efficacy and confidence in your area of expertise. May your life be filled with happiness!

more confident than those who are disorganized. If you want to build self-confidence and achieve a world of success in your work and life, incorporate organization in everything you do.

Disorganized people are always busy reprimanding themselves because of their failures; consciously or unconsciously, this destroys self-confidence.

Therefore, strengthen your self-confidence with organization in everything that you do, for organization builds character and shines brilliant light on your beliefs and self-confidence. May you be organized in all that you do!

Principle 25: The Principle of Avoiding Procrastination

Procrastination is the silent killer of success in life. People who always put off until tomorrow what they can do today are single-handedly designing their own failure. Successful people do tasks without delay and in a timely manner.

After you commit to doing something, every time you think about doing it but don't, you automatically reprimand yourself and your subconscious mind for not completing the task. This essentially scars your self-confidence and self-efficacy.

Sometimes, by procrastinating and postponing something, a person may lose the essence of an opportunity. As the Persian poet Nezami Ganjavi put it, "In delaying, there are disasters hidden."[5] With an organized plan in your life, may you do all your tasks in a timely manner and stop procrastinating.

Success requires punctuality, and the structure of your character has a direct relationship to how sensitive you are toward planning various matters in your life and how much importance you give them. As the saying goes, "If it's not a big deal, then please do it now." Stop making excuses to put things off until later.

The only thing that you are allowed to put off is procrastination! Your success in life relies on executing your tasks in a timely manner. Your self-confidence depends on refraining from procrastination.

Principle 26: The Principle of Managing Time

People who enjoy high self-confidence usually hold firm the reins of their wild horse of time, and they steer and manage their time well. People who waste their time always have a feeling of being behind and unable to catch up.

Those who manage their time well experience a boost in confidence. How are you dealing with your time? Do you effectively manage your time? Do not rest your head at night until you have exactly planned out how you will spend the next twenty-four hours.

Some people are careless about the passing of their valuable time, each moment of which can be used to achieve a success. A conscious individual like you is constantly mindful of time and manages it well.

You must plan for every twenty-four hours of your life. You should also have a plan for your weeks, months, and years. Watch out for time-thieves. Pointless telephone calls and prolonged, unproductive conversations can rob you of your time. Be mindful of your time and enjoy the fact that you manage it well based on a plan to help you create a world of confidence in yourself. May your lifetime be long and your time here be productive.

Principle 27: The Principle of Managing Priorities

Throughout your life and career, many responsibilities and tasks must be carried out during the day or week, month or year. One way to be successful is to prioritize your responsibilities. In any case, time is limited and sometimes there is more to do than time to do it. In this situation, determining which tasks have a higher priority will allow you to complete at least the most important ones. This simple act also improves your self-confidence.

Principle 28: The Principle of Not Comparing Yourself to Others

One of the main culprits that diminish self-confidence is the act of comparing yourself to others. People who constantly look at the accomplishments of others and lose sight of their own greatness and abilities unwittingly destroy their self-confidence.

People who believe in themselves hold themselves in high esteem. On the other hand, when people compare themselves to others and say, "How lucky is *that* person! Why can't I be that lucky?" the subconscious mind is influenced and assumes that they are in fact a "nobody," incapable of the achievements of others. The foundation of self-confidence is damaged.

As a successful student of the Technology of Thought, you never compare yourself with another. Rather, you draw your attention to the fruitful future that you have designed for yourself. You always tell yourself, "I will be lucky within six months!" or "I will be lucky in one year!" and ultimately, "How lucky I have been in the past few years, since I have reached all of my life's goals. I am a happy and blessed person. I manifest my existence in the world and take delight in it."

Tap into Your Thoughts

When you compare your current self to your future self, your subconscious mind creates the best life possible, boosting your self-confidence. Do not think that you are incapable of doing what others are capable of doing. Rather it is you who, by planning and designing a beautiful future, is able to achieve success in all areas of your life. Believe in yourself so that the world believes in you, and know that what you believe is what you will see occur in reality. It is not that you must see it to believe it—believe it to see it!

Principle 29: The Principle of Having Goals and a Life Plan

There are two types of people in the world: those who have goals and know what they want in life and have already visualized their future, who travel along the path of life with a world of confidence; and those who do not have any specific goals in life, who move through life scattered and without a plan. They do not have any dreams and don't know what they want. These aimless people are usually lost on the path of life and are typically far from a bright future.

Self-confidence has a direct relationship with having a goal and a life plan. Ambitious people usually believe in themselves, while people who have no goals believe in themselves less and have less confidence.

Which type of person are you? Do you have a goal in life? Have you designed an appropriate plan for your future? Have you envisioned your life's plan? Do you have any dreams for your future?

Ultimately, goals determine the outcome and path of your life. It is goals that give an individual self-confidence and motivation to achieve greater heights. Set a goal for yourself in life, and do not wait around for others to make it happen!

Principle 30: The Principle of Gestures and Body Language

People who have high self-confidence usually show it in their outward appearance, standing out from the crowd. They speak firmly and confidently, holding their heads up high. Their stride is more purposeful and their pace more brisk. A person's gestures and body language have a direct relationship to the self-confidence he or she projects.

Do you notice your gestures and body language? How do you sit? How do you walk? When you speak with others, where do you look? (Directly into the other person's eyes?) Remember to project outward, and use body language that makes you appear to be confident. Make eye contact and be sure to stand tall, so that all eyes are upon you! With these thirty principles, forge ahead and move onward to a wonderful life filled with your newfound self-confidence!

6

COMMUNICATION IS THE
GOLDEN KEY TO SUCCESS

*O*ne day, I was sitting in my office at the University of Southern California (USC). Finals were fast approaching, and students were stopping by my office for extra help. As each student entered my office, one after another, my attention was suddenly drawn to the way in which they entered my room! It was precisely their attitude and enthusiasm that unconsciously caused me to answer their questions with genuine interest and fondness, rather than just go through the motions.

After observing their manner, the way they greeted me, how they sat, and how they asked their questions, I made some interesting observations, which I'd like to share with you. Some of the students would enter and quickly jump to the issue at hand, ask their questions, anxiously await the answers, then rush to leave. Others would greet me and shake hands, expressing genuine enthusiasm for learning. These students would sit down, smiling, and engage in conversation first, before rattling off their list of questions. They'd say something that altered my frame of mind. One of them asked, "Dr. Azmandian, isn't it a beautiful day with perfect weather and clear skies?" Another said, "I am really grateful that you teach class in such an engaging manner and in a way that makes the material easy to understand. I just have a few additional questions about the material." Students who were better communicators were much more successful in obtaining the answers to their questions.

When my students communicate eloquently with me, I don't feel as though I'm just going through the motions; I don't get tired of providing detailed explanations. On the contrary, I thoroughly enjoy interacting with them. This is why communication is referred to as the "golden key to success." Great success begins with great communication.

HOW TO BE AN EFFECTIVE COMMUNICATOR

We are naturally social beings, and whatever task we accomplish and whatever achievement we pursue becomes, in some way, associated with other people. Therefore, a key factor in your success is establishing rich relationships with others, through communication. The Technology of

Thought system asserts that communication is the most important factor in our success.

The wealthiest people in the world are those who are able to establish better connections with others. The best managers are the ones who are successful at creating productive human relationships. Successful military commanders are people who are able to communicate their plans effectively. Great teachers are those able to reach their students. Successful parents are parents who can establish effective communication with their children.

When we talk about effective communication, we are referring to both personal communication and communication in a professional context. Communication is an art, and a person who communicates effectively is an artist. You need to communicate with creativity and ingenuity to be memorable, well-liked, and to be able to win people over.

"Communication is the conveying of emotions or information from one person to another." Based on this definition, communication has two very important pillars. The first pillar is the emotion in your heart or the information that you want to convey. The second pillar is how you convey it. The success of a communication depends on both elements together.

Communicate from the Heart

Successful communication spans people's hearts. When you want to establish rapport with someone, you transfer an emotion or information from one heart to another. The important thing to understand is that each heart has its own complexities. One way to look at it is this: on each person's heart there is a lock that requires a code to open it; successful communication takes place when the code is found, the lock opened, and you gain entry into another's heart and establish a connection. When you communicate with someone from the heart, they tend to respond better to what you're saying.

Of course, the issue is not just to open the door to a heart, but rather, having opened the door, it is about painting a beautiful picture on the canvas of the heart—remember, communication is an art form!

When communicating with others, it is best to put yourself in the other person's shoes. Think about how someone might react to what you're saying. The transfer of an emotion to another person requires a foundation that needs to be carefully built by the one initiating the conversation. For example, you may give someone a single rose, a symbol of love, affection, and intimacy, and be met with a pleasant reaction. However, you might give that same rose to someone else for whom it evokes bitter memories. Each person may react differently. You need to tailor your mode of communication to the individual, because an approach that is successful with one person may not be with another.

Tap into Your Thoughts

Think about the way you communicate. Be confident and make sure your method for communication has the ability to unlock hearts. People who believe in themselves are able to create beautiful connections by having powerful conversations. A beautiful and effective communicator requires a boldness and bravery that only self-confident individuals possess.

Remember that everyone has their own set of individual qualities. Many disputes stem from just these complexities and from a lack of mutual understanding and comprehension. Successful communication requires awareness and understanding of how another person will react.

Three Communication Styles:
Visual, Auditory, and Tactile

People can be classified as three kinds of communicators. Some people are "visual," and a successful way to communicate with them is through what they see while their other communication channels may be closed. Another group of people are "auditory," meaning that you can successfully communicate through what they hear. The third group is "tactile," meaning they normally establish communications through physical contact.

Of course, this does not mean that a person will communicate in a visual, auditory, or tactile way exclusively, but rather that he or she may have an affinity for one style over another. Being cognizant of the communication styles of others is the first step to successful communication. Here are some additional tips for effective communication.

SMILE. There is a saying: "Smiling is the first step in kindness." Whenever you meet people with a smile, you unlock their hearts. Some people, even those who don't have a particular problem, always frown, and they become unapproachable. So when you are alone, practice smiling, and know that smiling paves the way for successful communication, especially with those who are visual communicators.

GIVE A COMPLIMENT. An effective way to begin communication with someone who is inclined to auditory communication is to open with a compliment. Most people like to be the object of other people's admiration. Praising someone will not only build his or her self-confidence, it will also cause that person to have a great feeling toward you.

WRITE A LETTER. Another good technique that promotes effective communication is letter writing (or e-mail). Most of the things that people cannot express in person, they can better express in a letter. Therefore, if you get in the habit of writing letters, not only will you be able to solve many of your own existing communication problems, you will also deeply touch the recipient with your words.

When writing a letter, pay attention and adhere to two very important principles. First, in the beginning of the letter, speak highly of the other person in a very honest and genuine manner. Second, express your true intention for the written communication. For example, say you have a business associate who constantly hassles you, someone you don't get along with. Here's an example of a letter you could write to him to open up communication:

> Dear [colleague], you are an exceptional person, and I have always admired your knowledge and expertise. I especially admire the kind attitude you take with your clients. I must say that I am proud to have a colleague like you. . . . I believe that regarding this matter [the problem between you], it might be better for our working relationship if we were to work toward a resolution.

Surely, when your colleague receives such an honest letter from you, he will be moved and will realize that he made a mistake in his behavior toward you. The letter would undoubtedly lead him to reconsider his thoughts and behavior, and from now on he will act friendly toward you. You will enjoy associating and working with him, and eventually the quality of your life will improve because of this simple method of communication. This is the nature of good communication, which can ultimately enrich your life and make you successful in all that you do.

Remember, effective communication is a very important factor in elevating the quality of your life, and it allows you to reach the highest levels of success, acquiring wealth, spirituality, knowledge, and other achievements of a good life. Establish communication, win people's hearts, and enrich your life.

7

SET GOALS AND DESIGN
YOUR DESTINY

*A*mbition is the catalyst that prompts people to act.
Ambitious people set goals for their life and strive to achieve
them with enthusiasm and excitement. It is ambition that
propels one along the path of life toward one's goals. A
person without ambition is like a traveler who is lost in the
desert of life on a dark night, going around in circles, not
getting anywhere.

Goals shine light on your path to success and give
meaning to actions. People without goals will not get anywhere because they have nothing to strive for. The difference between having something and not having it is desire,
and desire springs from a great goal. Now let's take a closer
look at effective goal setting and how we can design the
future we want.

Before we continue, let me ask you a few questions: Do you have goals? Do you know exactly what kind of future awaits you? Have you designed your future? If you answered yes to these questions, then you're on track; if you answered no, then now is the time to think about your goals and plans for your life.

RESEARCH: POSITIVE EFFECTS OF SETTING GOALS

In 1953 at Yale University, a group of researchers decided to study and analyze the phenomena of ambition and setting goals. Their experiment examined people with and without goals and how this difference affected them.

Researchers studied subjects who had successfully received their undergraduate degree that year. The graduates were asked whether they had set any specific career and life goals. Only 3 percent of these graduates said that, indeed, they had mapped out their futures for themselves. The remaining 97 percent said they did not have any clear goal for their life. The researchers followed the lives of these graduates for twenty years. After twenty years, in 1973, researchers went back to the graduates and asked the questions, "What have you accomplished during these past twenty years? How much money have you made?" After receiving answers, the researchers proceeded to analyze the results and were surprised to find that the accomplishments of the 3 percent who had goals were greater than the combined accomplishments of the remaining 97 percent who did not have any future goals. The reason for the success of the 3 percent was what they had in common: goals and a life plan. You can be sure that successful people everywhere are like that 3 percent: they planned their future in advance.

Goals clarify the destination and path of a life. Would you like to design a beautiful future for yourself and specify your goals in life? Would you like to be seen as an ambitious individual who has a plan in life? Would you like to be able to just think and create? To generate a hurricane of success? To live with pride and honor? Do you want to do something divine in your life? By planning and setting goals, do you want to specify the entire path of your life, producing a masterpiece?

After reading this chapter, you will be able to do all of these things and more, but first I would like you to take part in a special ceremony called the "Night of Designing Destiny" ceremony. During this beautiful ceremony, I would like you to do something that was done by the Lord one night, called God's "Night of Designing Destiny."

THE "NIGHT OF DESIGNING DESTINY" CEREMONY (EXPANDING THE ACCOMPLISHMENTS OF LIFE)

The formation of existence by the Lord was based on the philosophy of planning and setting goals. There was a time when nothing existed in the entire universe except for God. At some point in time, the Lord planned and designed all of the creatures in existence and named this event the "Night of Designing Destiny." Afterward, God created the entire universe.

All of the beauty in the world is due to the designing done on that special "Night of Designing Destiny." This shows that the design of any phenomenon has the most important role in the quality of its creation.

Such nights of destiny can occur in the life of any beautiful individual, like you. In other words, you can design, manage, and plan the entire future of your life in one sacred night. If you put effort into such a beautiful and fateful movement, you will begin the process of arranging and designing a future that bears no resemblance to your past. A future filled with success, tranquility, wealth, knowledge, excellence, spirituality, and thousands of other accomplishments worthy of you.

The Importance of the "Night of Designing Destiny"

The occurrence of the "Night of Designing Destiny," the designing of fate, should take place in a beautiful and special ceremony. This act creates belief in you and inserts a powerful and prolific signal into your subconscious mind, producing a wonderful result in your world.

You now know well that for a beautiful person transformed by the Technology of Thought, it is important to utilize the capabilities of the subconscious mind in achieving goals. With the explanation and comparisons that were made regarding this powerful phenomenon inside you, we reached the conclusion that your subconscious is like a small child that, on one hand, naïvely looks at you to see what you intend to say and what command you are going to give. And on the other hand, it holds supernatural powers that can contribute to the destruction or construction of your life, beliefs, goals, and so on.

Therefore, your entire focus should be directed toward your subconscious mind and how you handle it and what you say to it. Along these lines, executing the "Night of Designing Destiny" conveys to your subconscious mind that this matter is completely serious and definite, that your subconscious mind should pay attention to its vital responsibility and put all its efforts into creating your wonderful goals.

So conduct this beautiful ceremony with love and spiritual and emotional observance so that you achieve the most amazing results.

How to Perform the "Night of Designing Destiny" Ceremony

As you know, when your thoughts and emotions become entwined, they create a powerful signal that is transmitted to your subconscious mind. Therefore, in order to execute your "Night of Designing Destiny" ceremony, you must understand that this is a divine opportunity that the Lord has provided for you, to act as God and to accomplish whatever you set out to achieve. At the same time, the entire quality of your future life depends on what you ask for on this night. Whatever you ask on this night will be created for you in your future (Ask and you shall receive). So you see how this night is of particular and great importance in your destiny.

In other words, how and under what circumstances your tomorrow and the days that follow it are spent all depend on what you asked for on this night. The Generous Lord will guarantee the achievement of all of your beautiful goals, provided that they are accompanied by your efforts and hard work.

On this divine, spiritual night, you invite God to attend your "Night of Designing Destiny" ceremony and He orders the entire universe to act under your command and congregate in this beautiful heavenly/human assembly and gather around you and bear witness to your beautiful future destiny—the same future that is planned by you and which is destined by the Lord. A narrative explains, "God's believer does the planning and God destines for it to happen."

You should now proceed to design your destiny and live out your beautiful future in a state of love and emotion and with complete hope and belief. It is important that you be prepared for your "Night of Designing Destiny," which has such vital significance in your fate. You should be prepared both on the outside and within your heart. First take a bath and then, with a cleansed body and mind, purify your intentions. Next, proceed to design your future and specify your goals. In the following sections, we will go over specific ways to promote goal setting on this night.

HOW TO SET GOALS

Your beautiful feelings of greatness and ability send powerful signals to your subconscious mind that help you achieve your most ambitious goals. Your efforts and the power of your subconscious mind are the means to your success.

Step 1: List Your Goals

Before anything else, you should prepare a list of all the goals you would like to achieve.

List every single goal you have, whether emotional, spiritual, financial, or career-specific—all kinds. Include all of your life's goals, the attainment of which you would be content with for the rest of your life. At this moment, as you are thinking about the goals themselves, do not think of how you will go about trying to achieve them—that part of the process comes later.

Step 2: Schedule Your Goals

Once you have an actual list of things to strive for, you can create a timeline for when you would like to accomplish these goals. For each goal, specify a period of time for completion; a goal without a time constraint does not have value.

A person values a goal only when he or she sets a specific time to achieve it. Setting a time frame is a sign that you are committing to that goal. Hold yourself responsible to attain your goals within the time constraints you have assigned. Obviously, the assigned time frame for each goal is an estimate, which you must make based on your belief in your capabilities, situation, and environmental conditions.

Of course, it may be the case that a goal is attained before its predetermined date and time, or that in order to achieve a goal some more time is needed, in which case you should not be discouraged. You need to be flexible with your schedule.

Step 3: Prioritize Your Goals

In this step, it is necessary for you to refer to your list of time-associated goals and organize them according to their priority. Priorities can be based on the date and time of the goal or on its importance. In any case, we clarify and illuminate these issues for our subconscious mind.

Step 4: Create Motivation for Each Goal

The achievement of any goal requires motivation and effort. Motivation is the process of persuading ourselves and our subconscious mind to complete the goals before us. With this step, you should write down at least two paragraphs answering "Why?" Why is it important for you to achieve this goal? This reflection is called the Power of *Why*. If you understand the reasons driving you to accomplish a specific goal, you will attribute meaning and motivation to work hard for each and every achievement.

Step 5: Set Plans to Achieve Goals

Having a plan for how to reach each goal is one of the requirements for achieving it. Without a plan, where do you begin? You do not necessarily need to stick to your original plan to attain your goal, however. As you work to accomplish a particular goal, your subconscious mind may offer better solutions along the way. Therefore, allow some flexibility as you work toward your goals.

With the help of your subconscious mind, your long journey will result in the greatest accomplishments of your life.

Step 6: A First Move

This step, which you will perform on the day following your "Night of Designing Destiny," is to make a small first move toward achieving each goal. For example, let's say one of your goals on your "Night of Designing Destiny," is to buy a beautiful car within the next two years. On the day after your "Night of Designing Destiny," at an appropriate time and with complete seriousness, you should go to an elegant car dealership and act like a person who has thousands of dollars in his or her pocket and would now like to buy the ideal car—minus the last part where you actually pay the money. Of course, your belief is that you will get to that part in two years when you achieve the necessary financial goal.

This serious move conveys to your subconscious mind that the "Night of Designing Destiny" ceremony and designing your own fate is a completely serious, logical, and feasible act. Each of your moves and actions are powerful signals that enter your subconscious and create power within you, giving you the motivation that "Yes, you can!" This type of life and these types of hope-inspiring actions are the sustenance of the subconscious mind. They create beautiful beliefs and powerful motivations to help achieve the future goals of a wonderful life belonging to you. Live happily and work hard.

HOW TO ACHIEVE PLANNED GOALS

The following principles provide guidelines to help you reach your goals.

Principle 1: Set Your Plan in Motion

Certainly the first principle toward achieving a goal is working hard for it—taking action and setting your plan in motion. Goals are achieved through effort, and successful people are those who work hard, even tirelessly.

As the eloquent thirteenth-century Persian poet Sadi[1] has said, "Without enduring strife, no treasure is achieved." Of course in this poem, from the point of view of a follower of the Technology of Thought, the word "strife" means motion and effort, not pain and struggle. Those who have been transformed by the Technology of Thought define their world in such a way that they enjoy every second of their life, as much as possible.

So, hard work and effort create a world of enthusiasm in you, because they result in your reaching the goal you set. From this, we can conclude that it is great for people to choose a career they love, as it will lead them to more successes. People who settle for a job where each second feels like torture, and try to justify the situation by saying they have no choice and can't find a better job, should know that they are greatly mistaken. You *can* reevaluate your life goals, set new ones, and set into motion a better life for yourself.

Principle 2: Using the Power of Thought and the Power of the Subconscious Mind

In addition to setting your plans in motion to strive toward your goal, you must also use your supernatural ability through the power of thought and the power of the subconscious mind.

A person's subconscious mind, besides having the responsibility of creating beliefs and self-confidence, has another very important mission, and that is communicating with the world's infinite intelligence and assembling all the means necessary for achieving one's desired goals. The question is, can all humans use this supernatural ability? Only those who give their subconscious the proper signals can unlock its source of infinite power.

When you are constantly aware of this infinite power you possess, guide it by sending positive and constructive messages. As you know, the most important input for your subconscious mind is your thoughts at each moment. Every train of thought that you create with absolute hope and emotion is by itself an energy source that resonates throughout the world. As with other laws of nature, this energy can definitely be turned into matter (a materialized goal), making your wishes and dreams a reality. People who think positively and optimistically reach their goals. People who think negatively and pessimistically, as you would expect, don't reach their goals. Each positive word causes you to use the infinite power of your subconscious mind.

Program the Subconscious to Achieve Goals

Think about your subconscious mind as a computer. The input signals to your subconscious are received through your five senses and your thoughts. Your ability to control these input signals is what makes the accomplishments of the subconscious great. The output of the subconscious mind results in a positive mental outlook, confidence, and the ability to communicate with the world's infinite intelligence to achieve your beautiful goals.

Remember, one of the ways to send productive signals to the subconscious mind is through the use of positive affirmations. Meaning, every positive sentence that you say, write, or read about yourself is an effective signal to the subconscious. Examples of positive affirmations are as follows. You must fully believe in these mantras as you repeat them, because they will transform your thoughts:

I am a successful and happy individual.

Every day I become more healthy and beautiful.

In my world, everything is different.

From the sky, blessings always rain down on me.

Every day, money and wealth are drawn toward me.

I live in a world of spirituality and divine love.

I am a wealthy and powerful human being.

Wealth, health, spirituality, and tranquility are the
     assets of my life.

I am a lucky person.

I am the masterpiece of creation.

I am always cheerful and smiling.

Wherever I am, I always look for beauty.

My life is completely geared toward excellence.

All difficulties in my book of life can be solved.

I have faith in my ability to reach my goals.

> I am an attractor of wealth and a magnet for success
> and happiness.
>
> Each day, more so than the day before, I experience a
> deluge of divine blessings upon me.

Every affirmation that you express with strong belief and emotion is a powerful signal that compels your subconscious to create that exact reality for you.

VISUALIZATION: A POWERFUL METHOD TO ACHIEVE GOALS

A computer can be provided with either discrete, limited data or a scan of an entire image. Just as the saying goes, "A picture is worth a thousand words," an image provides much more information to the computer than discrete data. This variation in terms of input is also true for the subconscious mind (your internal computer). In addition to using positive affirmations, where only limited information is sent to your subconscious, you can also send more complete images—which at times might be more effective.

Visualization is a powerful technique whereby you create a mental image of yourself fulfilling your goals. Mental images can convey a wealth of information to your subconscious mind. When you visualize your successes, your subconscious will actualize those mental images so that your goals materialize (when you visualize, you material-

Tap into Your Thoughts

Always envision your goals as though they have already been fulfilled. See yourself as successful, as someone who has been able to achieve goals. Believe what you imagine in your mind. Be certain that whatever you believe, you will see in reality. We have always heard people say, "I will believe it when I see it." *But, you must believe it in order to see it.*

ize). For instance, if one of your goals is to buy a beautiful car, you can visualize yourself having purchased your ideal car. This mental image, when repeatedly sent to the subconscious, lays the foundation for your dreams to become a reality. You will one day find yourself driving your own car—the exact image of which you had envisioned in your mind. This is the power of mental visualization, a great method for programming your subconscious mind.

8

SOLVE LIFE'S PROBLEMS
SUCCESSFULLY

I hope you have begun using the principles of the
Technology of Thought within your own life to transform
and become more successful. You have but one mission in
life: *to enjoy every moment of your life*. Moments of thinking
and creating beautifully, moments of believing in yourself
and your abilities, moments of designing and creating your
destiny and future, moments of happiness and successful
endeavors. However, it takes a bit of work to achieve *your*
ideal life.

We live in the world of realities and not ideals. For us,
the real world is filled with problems and life's challenges—
challenges we face every day and over which we don't
always have control. These problems and difficulties can
have an effect on our quality of life.

We can't escape our problems. The only remedy is to handle them successfully by becoming transformed by the Technology of Thought. You can face life's problems, solve them powerfully and skillfully, and enjoy every moment of your life. As we come across each problem, we should face it with the mentality that we will not allow it to harm our soul, mind, and spirit.

CONSIDER LIFE'S CHALLENGES AS HIDDEN BLESSINGS

Since your life is ruled by your belief system, the events in your life should occur along the same lines as your beautiful beliefs and thoughts. This means that in your world, no events unfold that can cause you harm or damage your quality of life.

With this philosophy, it becomes clear that, for a person who is transformed by the Technology of Thought, seemingly unpleasant occurrences often reveal themselves as blessings in disguise. We must put aside the unpleasant exterior of our life's challenges and find their inner value, and in this manner make the quality of our life more wonderful.

Thus, problems in your life are actually blessings hidden inside unpleasant packaging. Your intelligence and awareness dictate that you find what's positive about your situation and benefit from it.

A life without problems can be disastrous. How? There are numerous examples of people who have everything, living in the lap of luxury, without any problems or a care in the world, yet who are still unhappy and unsatisfied. This is because without problems or challenges, people become stagnant. Challenges and hardships breathe spirit and excitement into life. They are a wake-up call; people only realize the value of their life when they are faced with challenges.

Encountering life's difficulties also polishes and shines the pearl of one's existence, building character and strength. Meeting challenges increases self-efficacy. Have you ever noticed that prominent and successful people are those who, more than others, have encountered difficulties and problems in their life, solved them, and become successful?

Comfort Zone

As we think about self-efficacy and improving our ability to solve problems, think of yourself in the center of a circle, your "comfort zone." The radius of this circle depends on your capacity to cope with adversity. People who have a vast comfort zone are very calm when faced with problems. They are extremely positive, never become anxious, and they greatly enjoy their lives.

If an event that happens to someone occurs within this circle, it will have no unpleasant effect on the person. On the other hand, if an event happens for someone outside of his or her comfort zone, it is regarded as a problem or

Tap into Your Thoughts

Any problem in life can be considered an opportunity for advancement and improvement, an opportunity to learn from experience. Overcoming life's challenges builds character, strengthening our ability to confront future problems. Keep in mind the saying "When you succeed, you party, and when you fail, you ponder."

obstacle for the person, causing him or her to lose morale and become extremely anxious. The more often you encounter problems that you are able to solve, the larger the circle of your comfort zone becomes.

Therefore, problems actually have the potential to increase your capacity to handle them, to enlarge your comfort zone. This makes your outlook on life grander. Ultimately, you become like a mountain, standing firm and upright against life's problems, solving them, and enjoying every moment of life.

HOW TO CONFRONT AND SOLVE PROBLEMS

Though problems can be considered hidden blessings, we still need to learn how to overcome them. What separates you from other people who are unable to confront challenges is your ability to use your subconscious mind. As a successful student of the Technology of Thought, you believe that you must take control of your subconscious and harness all of its infinite power to assist you. Your subconscious, without any judgment, listens to your every command to see what you will say and how you will guide it.

Therefore, your talent lies in your ability to guide your subconscious mind. The principles that follow refer to this characteristic of the subconscious mind. By following them, you will guide your subconscious to assist you with solving your problems.

Principle 1: Change Your Outlook About Problems

As mentioned earlier, problems can contain hidden gems of blessings, but oftentimes, our outlook on a problem is negative and limited. We may even think that we're being tortured or punished. On the contrary, we shouldn't think of an obstacle as punishment, but as an "opportunity in disguise" for us to experience, solve, and grow from.

Therefore, our perspective on life's difficulties is one of opportunity, sometimes even a golden opportunity, to successfully pass through a gauntlet of tests and emerge successful. Having this outlook definitely plays a significant role in guiding our subconscious mind, creating hope and resolve within us.

Principle 2: Use Positive Words

You now know very well that every word you use has a specific impact on your subconscious mind. When you say, "I am exhausted," the word *exhausted* leaves an unpleasant impression on the subconscious, subsequently making you more exhausted, and frustrated because of your exhaustion.

When a person says, "I am tranquil," the word *tranquil* is processed in the subconscious mind and produces a tranquil spirit within that individual. If a person says, "I am defeated," the word *defeated* creates a tired and broken spirit in the subconscious mind. If instead, the person had said, "I gained an experience," the word *experience* would for the subconscious mind suggest the concept of learning a lesson and would not only *not* weaken the spirit, but it would create a hopeful and happy one.

In addition to looking at a problem from a different perspective, it's also important to stay away from negative words that perpetuate your unfortunate situation. Use positive words to define the experience. Never say, "What an unfortunate situation we are in!" or "What a disaster!" or "Why do I always have the worst luck?" Instead, be cautious with your words and say, "A problem has occurred for me that I will solve, and I will be successful."

The words *difficulty* and *problem* might seem to have the same meaning, but for the subconscious mind the difference is like night and day. This is because, for the subconscious mind, the word *difficulty* conveys the sense of an extremely complicated phenomenon, which may even be unsolvable. The word *problem*, on the other hand, connotes a very different meaning for your subconscious mind; it knows that a "problem" has a solution.

This is why a person transformed by the Technology of Thought is particularly cautious with the words he or she uses, especially when problems arise at work and in life. That is when you will utilize your subconscious mind's endless power.

Principle 3: Remembrance, Reliance, and Trust in God or a Higher Power

When confronting problems, above all else, people need hope, protection, and support from a powerful source. They need to establish a spiritual connection with whatever higher being they believe in, be it God, the universe, or another source. When a person asks for assistance and knows that a higher power seeks to help, he or she has a reinforced sense of hope and is able to tackle the problem with complete optimism and confidence.

Principle 4: Self-Confidence and Self-Assurance

Self-confidence and self-assurance are very important factors in the successful confrontation of life's problems. People who believe in themselves stand like a mountain in the face of life's problems and solve them—and they delight in

Tap into Your Thoughts

When you believe in and know you can rely on God or a higher power, you feel protected, and you have the resolve and courage to stand strong when faced with obstacles in life, allowing you to easily overcome any problem.

their ability to do so. Remember to believe in yourself; it is important for creating a strong and resilient spirit.

You are a person made remarkable with the Technology of Thought. You have created your belief system anew, and on this beautiful foundation you have built self-confidence. As such, when you encounter a problem, visualize yourself overcoming it. With your thoughts, find your solution.

Principle 5: Think "How?" Instead of "Why?"

When faced with unpleasant events, unsuccessful people tend to complain, constantly asking, "Why? Why did this disaster happen to me? Why am I so unfortunate? Why am I always a failure? Why . . . ?" When you think in terms of *why*, you unknowingly destroy your spirit, and your subconscious hits a dead end. Not only does it accept failure, but it also makes no effort to solve the problem. As a result, you remain helpless and get nowhere.

In contrast, the most integral word upon which success hinges is *how*. Successful, happy people constantly ask themselves, "How? How can I best solve my problems? How can I establish meaningful relationships? How can I achieve my goal? How can I design a wonderful future for myself? How . . . ?"

One very important principle for solving life's problems is asking questions, but you need to ask the right questions, *how* questions, so that you can work toward solving the problem.

Principle 6: Golden Questions

By understanding the subconscious mind and how it works, we know the effect that questions have on it—especially the right kinds of questions.

When faced with problems at work and in life, the way we confront them and the types of questions we ask ourselves are extremely important. The quality of your life is determined by the type of questions you ask yourself.

When an individual transformed by the Technology of Thought faces a problem, while preserving all of the rules and principles of handling problems, that person must ask himself or herself at least four fundamental questions, as suggested by Anthony Robbins. Posing these questions will program your subconscious mind so that, in addition to creating within you a hopeful and tranquil spirit, its communication with the entire world of existence and all of creation will find the best solution and bring it to your attention.

Here are the four fundamental questions to reflect upon:

QUESTION 1: "WHAT POSITIVE MESSAGE DOES THIS EVENT HAVE FOR ME?" As you can see, this question is posed from a completely positive perspective, and each word in it conveys a positive signal to the subconscious mind, saying, "A disaster, problem, difficulty, or accident has not occurred to destroy my spirit or leave me helpless. Rather, this is just an experience for growth. Oh subconscious, search and discover what positive message this event has for me."

After receiving this question, the subconscious mind accepts that this incident or problem is not a disastrous occurrence but rather just an event for which it must search the entire universe, acquire its positive message, and convey it to you. Such a question stems from a place of power within us, not one of weakness and inability. Therefore, this question allows for the creation of a positive outlook by the subconscious mind.

QUESTION 2: "WHAT VALUABLE LESSON CAN I LEARN BY SOLVING THIS PROBLEM?" This question causes the subconscious mind to feel that the problem is one that can definitely be solved and, at the same time, lessons can be learned from it. Your subconscious mind will search for them. The subconscious must first instill a positive spirit within us, and then it will search for the appropriate solutions.

QUESTION 3: "WHAT MUST I DO TO SOLVE THIS PROBLEM ACCORDINGLY?" Through the subconscious mind, this question says, "I am not a slave to this problem, but instead, the problem is a slave to me. I am trying to figure out what I should do to solve the problem, rather than waiting to see what happens." This question takes you to a place of power and not a place of weakness. It means, "My problem is going to be solved and in the manner which I approve." Such productive, spirit-boosting questions create self-confidence.

QUESTION 4: "WHAT ACTIONS MUST I IMMEDIATELY TAKE SO THAT IN ADDITION TO SOLVING THIS PROBLEM, I ENJOY THE PATH TO A SOLUTION?" It seems that after the first three questions, it's time to take measures, decisions, and actions directed toward solving the problem. But those made beautiful by the Technology of Thought also want to feel good about the fact that they are solving their problem—they want to enjoy it. For example, if you were at first unsure that you would be able to solve your problem, you were upset and worried. But now that the problem is on its way to being solved, you can begin to enjoy yourself. Because you know that a problem has a solution and that you're working to solve your problem, confident you will succeed, there is no need to be anxious.

With complete faith that you are successfully solving your problem, enjoy the process from beginning to end.

Ultimate Success Formula for Solving Life's Problems

I want to introduce a formula that will help you solve every problem successfully. It is called the "Ultimate Success Formula," and it can be used to achieve anything (but it works particularly well for solving problems at work and in life). Here are the steps:

1. WE MUST KNOW EXACTLY WHAT WE WANT AND WHAT WE ARE AFTER AND FEEL AS THOUGH THE PROBLEM HAS ALREADY BEEN SOLVED. A lot of times, when facing problems and difficulties, people become overly nervous and worried. In our minds, we make the problem out to be bigger than it really is, creating fear and anxiety and causing us to become less capable of solving it.

The first requirement for solving life's dilemmas is to have an appropriate understanding of the problem at hand. You must clearly define the issue, know exactly what has occurred, and specify the extent of the problem.

When faced with a challenge, take a pen and a piece of paper and write down exactly what the situation is.

This accurate description of the problem is your "problem statement." Then ask yourself what it means to solve this problem. In other words, what must happen in your life for you to say that your problem has been solved? This action is called clarification.

2. FIND THE BEST SOLUTION AND IMMEDIATELY TAKE ACTION. As a successful individual, you know very well that taking action is the first step to solving problems and achieving goals. When faced with a challenge, we must not dwell on the problem statement or become too preoccupied with the problem. Rather, 80 percent of our time and energy should be spent on acting to solve the problem, with only 20 percent spent on expressing and explaining the problem statement.

3. EVALUATE ACTIONS TAKEN TO SOLVE A PROBLEM: CONTROL YOUR PATH, ALTER SOLUTIONS IF NECESSARY, AND SHOW FLEXIBILITY. Successful students of the Technology of Thought are always evaluating all phases of their life and actions in order to select the best path, make the greatest decisions, and achieve their goals. When faced with a problem, any action you take toward solving it you must immediately evaluate and analyze. And you need to be very flexible, so that you can change and alter your path to the solution as you go, finding the best solution in the best way possible.

Keep in mind that all along the path, your subconscious mind, which is continually in touch with all of creation, finds better solutions and brings them to your attention. Always be ready to receive your internal inspiration, and constantly seek out better solutions.

4. LEARN FROM THE EXPERIENCES OF OTHERS AND MAKE MODELS OF SUCCESSFUL PEOPLE. A conscious individual transformed by the Technology of Thought never uses trial and error to solve his or her problems. This is especially true during critical times and when making strategic and significant decisions, when using the experience of others can be very advantageous and bring us success. For any problem, always try to find a person who has faced a similar situation and dealt with it successfully. Follow his or her example; consult with your role model in order to find the shortest route to a solution.

5. MAINTAIN UNWAVERING FAITH AND OPTIMISM TOWARD A SOLUTION. Being in great spirits and having faith in the solution to a problem is the greatest asset you have when facing problems in life. A despondent person can never think correctly and will not find a suitable solution. As a successful person, you should believe that problems are an opportunity for you to grow and excel. Always stay optimistic so that you can solve each problem with your wisdom and intelligence. Enjoy your power.

Tap into Your Thoughts

Role models and the examples they provide are like bright lights that can illuminate the path of your life. Using the examples and experiences of others allows you to accomplish great things with the least possible expenditure of time and energy.

6. KEEP A DETAILED RECORD OF SUCCESSES AND PRAISE YOURSELF AS A SUCCESSFUL PERSON WHO CAN OVERCOME ANY CHALLENGE. Once you've overcome a challenge, take a moment to reflect on your ability to come to a successful resolution and to overcome adversity. The only thing left to do is to record your success and praise yourself! When faced with a problem, you solved it and transformed into a person with a great capacity for success and a larger comfort zone. Engrave this power into your soul; record your great success in your journal of successes.

9

CREATE LASTING CHANGES AND TRANSFORMATIONS

*C*hanging and transforming yourself to be successful through the Technology of Thought is only valuable if the transformation remains permanent. Consider the case of a person who, at one point in time, creates a transformation in himself. Then, after some time has passed, the results of that transformation diminish, causing him to revert back to his former self. Certainly, there is no point in putting effort into getting well if it is only going to be temporary.

At the first signs of transformation, you must not become complacent, thinking that this will last for the rest of your life, but rather, you must work to sustain a permanent transformation.

For example, a piece of iron that is placed inside a magnetic field for a while becomes a magnet. Then when its magnetic quality is used outside of the magnetic field, after a while, it slowly begins to lose its magnetism and goes back to being just a piece of iron. Therefore, it is necessary to place it back in a magnetic field so that it becomes a magnet again. Your inner being works the same way as that piece of iron. You need to place yourself back in the magnetic field of the Technology of Thought every once in a while to sustain your transformation.

HOW TO CREATE LASTING CHANGES AND TRANSFORMATIONS WITHIN OURSELVES

Now let us take a look at how we can systematically create a permanent and lasting transformation within ourselves. We will explain the principles of this system and show how by executing these principles you can keep your wondrous transformation permanent, increasing the power of your inner being day by day.

Principle 1: Practice the Techniques of the Technology of Thought

Your transformation is the result of the minute-by-minute awareness of the input signals (through your thoughts) fed to your subconscious mind. The most important factor for transformation is self-awareness. In other words, the most important action for you to take is to gain continual insight

into yourself; you must be aware that a significant event has occurred in your life and that you are no longer your old self, but instead, a whole new, successful person—someone who constantly practices all the techniques and principles of the Technology of Thought.

Therefore, do not neglect yourself for even one second. Be in a constant state of complete consciousness. Always focus on the beautiful aspects of your life, continually draw your attention to life's happy events, and refrain from any negativity. Ask yourself positive questions every day, and express your contentment toward life. And remember to always seek a better life for yourself. *At each and every waking moment, practice the Technology of Thought.*

Principle 2: Protect Your Subconscious Mind

The life you want to create for yourself relies on your subconscious mind, which determines the extent of your success, health, wealth, tranquility, spirituality, and all of your life's accomplishments.

You now know that your every thought, every action, and every sight you see affects the subconscious mind; the consequences of those effects can alter your destiny. Each input is a signal to your subconscious mind, the same signal that affects the well-being of your mind, soul, and future accomplishments. Your most important mission is caring for your subconscious mind and protecting it from harmful thoughts.

Tap into Your Thoughts

Whatever enters your subconscious mind through your five senses—beautiful flowers or rotting fruit, a cheerful song or a dirge—affects your destiny. It's important to take care of your subconscious mind so that it can take care of you, creating joy, happiness, and your future successes.

Principle 3: Find Mutual Support

Try to promote discussions on the Technology of Thought among your family members so that you all live together in a supportive Technology of Thought environment. People sometimes neglect themselves and say or do things that are contrary to the philosophy of the Technology of Thought. In such situations, it is very helpful to have mutual support—people who can give you quick reminders about your transformation.

When family and friends also decide to live by the principles of the Technology of Thought, they can act like guardians and teachers for one another so that none of them becomes neglectful. This prevents the effects of a transformation from fading and also strengthens the foundation of your belief system.

Principle 4: Use the Principles of the Technology of Love

To strengthen the beliefs of a transformed individual and to maintain a great spirit, practicing the principles of the Technology of Love is extremely effective and enjoyable. Remember, the Technology of Love refers to knowing that you are a special being, created and loved by a higher power. Through the Technology of Love, you see every phenomenon in existence as a manifestation of creation's greatness, and from this you take pleasure. This concept is a powerful signal for the subconscious mind and causes permanent transformation. A Technology of Love mindset constantly increases your "magnetic power" and recharges your "internal battery."

Principle 5: Set Goals and Create a Plan

Having a goal and a plan in life is one of the best ways for people to keep motivated, active, cheerful, and hopeful. It's exciting and transformation-inspiring.

People who constantly set new goals and design plans to reach their goals always see themselves on the path of excellence and transformation. These people do not have time to think about negative, destructive things and become depressed.

Ambitious individuals continually increase the intensity of their inner "magnetism." This is because they are always asking themselves, "How? How can I reach my goals? How can I successfully complete this project? How can I establish that communication?" Such inquisitive individuals always live blissfully.

Principle 6: Change Habits by Being Self-Aware

One of the best ways to keep your transformation permanent is to keep always aware by changing your habits and creating reminders for yourself that signal, "Indeed, I am no longer my former self, but rather, a transformed person whose reality has changed." If you do this you will have a permanent transformation, and you will never forget that the world has changed for you.

Every month, make a change in the decor of your home or workplace. Or change how you dress, the way you eat, or your interactions with others. Constantly change your entire life to manifest your internal change and transformation.

Principle 7: Use Positive Affirmations

Positive affirming sentences are a constructive command to your subconscious mind; they elevate your mood, and, in addition, form wonderful beliefs about your character. Positive affirmations set the foundation for the right conditions for your transformation. Fill your home and work environment with positive affirmations!

Principle 8: Imagine Success
Through Mental Visualization

Essentially, creating and imprinting positive images on your mind is a technique that provides a kind of blueprint for the subconscious, which allows an image to be realized in material form. Your subconscious mind causes your visions to become reality.

Mental visualization creates a wonderful feeling inside you; the subconscious mind communicates with all of creation and provides you with everything necessary to realize that mental image. Persistent and continuous mental visualization keeps your inner transformation permanent.

10

GAIN WEALTH
AND ABUNDANCE

*I*n the Technology of Thought, the word *wealth* has a broad and comprehensive meaning that includes any accomplishment in life. With this definition, everything that a person thinks and creates is a type of wealth. In other words, money is wealth. Knowledge is wealth. Spirituality and excellence are wealth. A successful marriage is wealth. Tranquility and joy are also wealth. With this comprehensive definition of wealth, let us now see how a student of the Technology of Thought can achieve abundance and what acts as the secret key to success in attaining wealth—in the true sense of the word.

Those who practice the Technology of Thought aspire to and achieve all kinds and definitions of wealth, most important, spiritual wealth, the significance of which we have touched upon again and again in these pages. In this chapter, we focus on how to acquire financial wealth. Financial wealth lets us enjoy material amenities, and it allows us to give more to others in need. It is one tool for achieving a great life.

Now the question is, how must a student of the Technology of Thought, for whom everything is different, utilize special rules in order to achieve wealth in the easiest and best way?

ACHIEVE WEALTH WITH THE TECHNOLOGY OF THOUGHT

There are certain principles that lead to the achievement of wealth and riches by a student of the Technology of Thought, which we describe here. Even though these sixteen principles can be applied toward the achievement of all kinds of wealth, our focus here is on methods to obtain money through lawful channels. To become wealthy, use the following tools:

Principle 1: Have a Wealth-Seeking Mindset

As you know, everything in your world begins with a thought. Wealthy individuals first create their wealth in their mind. People who have poor thoughts and a sense of poverty cannot achieve wealth. Basically, a person's thought is a type of energy that is generated in the factory of the mind and can turn into matter in the outside world. The nature of that matter depends exactly on the type of thought generated. Wealth-seeking thoughts are wealth-generating thoughts; this is a law of nature. A wealth-seeking mindset is established in a person only when he has a wealth-generating belief.

Therefore, before you begin to use your thoughts, take a look at your beliefs and see if you can picture yourself wealthy. At the same time, always remember that what you believe is what you will see. In order to create this belief in yourself, it is enough for you to note that most of the wealthy people in the world were once poor and underprivileged individuals who had no one to provide them with financial support and lend them a hand. These people had just one asset in their life, and that was belief in themselves. Certainly, if they had used mathematical equations rather than their beliefs to evaluate their financial prospects, they would have remained poor.

The equations of the world of existence are more complex than "two times two equals four." In order to achieve wealth, we must not see ourselves as slaves to these cut-and-dried formulas. The wealth we achieve has a direct relationship to our beliefs. Our beliefs help to determine the extent of our wealth.

The subconscious mind acts as a powerful system for gaining wealth or anything else we desire. Wealth-seeking thoughts and beautiful feelings that enter your subconscious mind combine to become an imperative to achieve financial wealth.

Essentially, the subconscious mind establishes communication with all of creation in order to see which factor or factors might be effective in achieving the wealth or financial goal you seek. A line from a beautiful poem by Sadi is applicable: "The clouds, wind, moon, sun, and entire universe are all busy working so that you obtain sustenance and do not live in ignorance."

Principle 2: Feel Wealthy and See Yourself in Complete Comfort, Then Give Charity

As you know, imagination and mental visualization have a strong influence on the subconscious mind. Therefore, people who sense themselves as being poor and are afraid of their financial situation will never become wealthy.

You should always try to see yourself as being wealthy and imagine that you are already provided ample sustenance. To the best of your ability, give charity so that your subconscious mind believes that you are actually wealthy and creates the conditions of a wealthy individual for you.

Always think about the infinite wealth that you are going to achieve in the future. Do not allow your birdlike thoughts to perch on branches of poverty and destitution. Always say, "I am wealthy," and because of this thought, express a great deal of gratitude for everything that you have. Act in such a manner that your subconscious mind truly senses your wealth and creates that exact situation for you in the world. Wealth-seeking feelings and thoughts generate wealth for you.

Feel your wealth and feel your comfort, and also remember to be charitable. Do not say, "I don't have, so I can't give." If you do, your subconscious mind will believe in your poverty and materialize that belief in your life. Therefore, give to charity, even if it is just a little. The extent of your charity is not very important to the subconscious mind; rather, the sheer act of giving is important, as it internalizes the belief that you are a wealthy individual.

Principle 3: "Ask and You Shall Receive"

There is a beautiful saying, "Ask and you shall receive." This is a remarkable sentence that applies to every stage and aspect of life. Requesting is the necessary condition for achieving. Although the Principle of Asking Questions usually applies in all situations, it is best to ask for success or even wealth and financial abundance from a more powerful entity, whether it is God, the universe, or any other higher power. Doing this evokes the philosophy, "Desire it, and it will happen."

When the subconscious mind receives a powerful command to obtain wealth, it acts as an initiator and searches the entire world of existence to see how it can achieve that goal in the best possible manner, the least amount of time, and with the easiest possible approach.

Principle 4: Love and Enjoy Money and Financial Abundance

The main requirement for achieving and creating a phenomenon to materialize before you is to love it. If you do not have a good feeling toward your intended goal, it is unlikely that you will easily achieve it. This general principle is also true with regard to acquiring wealth. For example, people who say "Money is dirty" or "The wealth of this world is nothing but trouble" cannot become wealthy.

There is another expression, "You lose what you condemn and you attract what you love." This principle reminds you that the condition for achieving a goal or accomplishment is to love it. Your subconscious mind's system essentially works in this manner. When you think about something and seek it, filled with emotion and passion, your subconscious receives a powerful command to strive toward achieving that desire, and, by coordinating with all of creation, it provides the means to create that desire in the physical world.

If you want to become wealthy based on this law of nature, you must feel affection toward money and wealth, regarding it as a great and beautiful tool and instrument, and passionately seek it out. Gaze upon symbols of wealth, like dollar bills, checks, images of bars of gold, and adore them and say, "Oh dollar bills, I will acquire millions and millions of you. I am fond of you, and I feel love for wealth as an instrument of success in life." This attitude toward symbols of wealth first of all gives you the feeling of being wealthy, and second, it sends a powerful command to your subconscious mind so that it strives toward achieving your financial and economic goals.

Principle 5: Specify the Range and Extent of Your Financial Desires

As you know, every goal must be completely specific, and the time frame within which to achieve it must be determined in advance. It is not enough to just say that you would like to become wealthy. You must determine the exact range and extent of the wealth and allocate a specific time frame in which to acquire it. For example, say, "I would like to acquire such-and-such amount of money within such-and-such amount of time."

Clarity of goals and the time frame within which to achieve them are very significant factors for the subconscious mind. Always try to give accurate and correct information to your subconscious, so that its mission becomes completely clear and it knows exactly what it should pursue and when it should achieve it. In the Technology of Thought, there is an expression that says, "Clarity is power." This concept applies exactly to your subconscious mind. Speak clearly with your subconscious through your thoughts, and express your requests very explicitly.

Principle 6: Plan to Achieve Wealth Within a Specified Time

You know that setting goals alone is not enough; rather, achieving a goal (wealth) within a specified time requires planning. If you are to acquire a certain amount of wealth in a specific time frame, you need to determine your path to success.

Remember to be flexible; recall that the plan and path for achieving a goal may actually change. By acquiring new information and experiences, individuals can arrive at better thoughts and find newer solutions for achieving their goals.

Aside from this, as soon as your subconscious mind receives a powerful input signal in the form of your desire to achieve a goal, it searches the world of existence in a continuous and constant manner, and by establishing a communication with all of creation, it discovers better solutions and brings them to your attention.

Therefore, in order to achieve your financial goals, some initial solutions are necessary, but this does not mean that you must follow them to the end. Rather, leave your mind open to welcome newer and better solutions that your subconscious brings to your attention; as a result, you will arrive at your destination much sooner.

Thus, flexibility along the path of reaching a goal is very important. Constantly alter your solutions so that you find the best ones.

Principle 7: Transform Large Figures into Smaller Figures with Shorter Time Frames and Await Initial Sprinklings

When your goal is a large sum of money and you have allocated a relatively large amount of time to achieve that great wealth, a doubt might form in your mind. You may think that attaining this large financial goal might be impossible for you—that it is out of reach and outside the realm of your beliefs. This negative and discouraging feeling may hinder you from working and striving to achieve such a goal. A much better solution is for you to transform large figures into smaller figures with shorter time frames. For example, select a very small and easily obtainable figure for yourself within a short time frame and make it your "financial goal number one." As soon as you meet this goal, a faith is instilled within you and your subconscious mind that you can easily arrive at your financial goals—that if you reached goal number one, you will definitely also reach subsequent goals. This becomes your belief, even if your subsequent goals are larger figures.

The important point is to create a hopeful belief and spirit in yourself that, "Indeed, I can achieve any reasonable financial goal." This becomes a huge motivator for you, so that you constantly strive and achieve wealth in a state of complete optimism and confidence.

Along these lines, it might interest you to know that one of the laws of humans in the world of existence is

Tap into Your Thoughts

You must anticipate initial sprinklings of wealth. Work hard and await them. For hardworking and optimistic individuals, they are only the beginning.

Always remember that long journeys begin with small steps. Therefore, consider every small step that you take on the path toward a goal a small success for yourself, and trust that it is the accumulation of small successes that leads you to a huge success, the achievement of your main goal.

that one must anticipate initial sprinklings. When initial sprinklings of wealth start to trickle down, a downpour of abundant wealth always follows. Just as the expression goes, "When it rains, it pours."

Principle 8: Constantly Take Action and Become a Wealth Magnet

Certainly, a person's accomplishments are achieved through action. Positive thoughts and a correct belief are necessary conditions to obtain what you want, but they are not sufficient in and of themselves. Constant effort to acquire wealth is necessary to reach your goal. What

Tap into Your Thoughts

Always think and say to yourself, "I am an attractor of wealth and a magnet to riches." This suggestion creates a more beautiful belief in you and gives your subconscious mind the energy and power to assist you in acquiring lawful wealth, allowing you to achieve your financial goals more quickly and easily.

Do not take for granted the small steps that you take to achieve your big goals. This is the law of success. Action, action, and more action. This is the secret to the success of great achievers throughout history. Treasure is just on the other side of action, and a wealth-seeking mindset is a map to the treasure. Beliefs are what discover the grains of gold in a wealth quarry, and action-producing thoughts are what extract them. Action is the factor that causes beliefs to bear fruit. Therefore, take action so that beliefs become prolific and ideas are realized.

makes your effort prolific are your feelings toward yourself and your belief in yourself as a "wealth magnet" who knows that with every one of your actions, dollar bills take flight toward you.

Principle 9: Believe in the Abundance of Blessings in the World and Trust That You Will Achieve Great Wealth

Essentially, stinginess and frugality act as barriers to wealth. The opposite of this is the belief that in the world of existence, there are ample blessings and that people create wealth themselves, increasing the wealth of the earth.

This concept is one of the laws of nature. You must believe that the vast earth is full of opportunities and it is up to humans to, without any limitation or exclusion, turn any opportunity into a wealth. Therefore, never think that the endeavors of others to achieve wealth could pose a threat to you.

The world of existence is full of wealth. Believe in this and know that you can achieve massive wealth. Pursue the other principles of attaining wealth, and do not hesitate for a moment.

Principle 10: Secure Your Best Interests Through Ensuring the Best Interests of Others

As Dr. Wayne Dyer puts it, "When you seek happiness for yourself, it will always elude you. When you seek happiness for others, you will find it yourself." People who only think about their own personal best interests less often have good fortune. I commend those people who, with complete broad-mindedness, request that others' needs are fulfilled before their own. Regarding this matter, if you participate in any cooperative effort, before all else, take care of the best interests of those around you so that your best interests are taken care of. You will be granted good fortune and blessings, and you will become wealthy.

Principle 11: You Must Enjoy What You Do, Otherwise Your Efforts Are in Vain

Many people forget this very important principle. They are willing to do any job, at any cost, without realizing that the main requisite of working and acquiring wealth is having tranquility and enjoying every moment of that job. If people are unhappy with what they do and spend all day in anguish and stress, all of their hard work is in vain. The main requisite of having a beautiful life is enjoying every moment of it. To achieve a life of bliss, your criterion for every effort should be based on this rule: *Do what you love and love what you do.* This guarantees that you avoid falling into the trap of a miserable life.

Remember that you are giving away the precious days of your life to your work, and you can never have those days back. Now think about what exactly you are being given in return. What good is wealth if it ends in a heart attack and all kinds of physical and mental problems? Remember that wealth is a means and not an end. It is an instrument for living, a tool for bringing about enjoyment, and a medium for giving to charity and excelling toward greatness.

If we make wealth our only goal and try to achieve it at all costs, we have completely lost. Be conscious and do not get trapped in just any job. Choose your job with complete awareness and consciousness, and make enjoying it your main and first priority.

Principle 12: Learn from Role Models Who Are Wealthy and Successful

When it comes to achieving goals, people can be divided into two groups. One group uses trial and error and, without consulting with experts or using any role models or examples, they take action. These people usually encounter difficulties in their work and make errors and mistakes; inevitably, they must correct their method and try again. Undoubtedly, acting in this manner requires spending more time, money, and energy and eventually results in a circuitous path to reaching a goal.

The other group, people who do the exact opposite, first consult with others and learn from the experiences of others. Essentially, to achieve any goal, they first seek out someone who has successfully accomplished this task before and make this person their example and role model. This way, they avoid the mistakes and learn from the successes of their role model, and ultimately, they achieve their great objectives most efficiently.

As a student of the Technology of Thought, avoid trial and error. Utilize examples and role models so that you achieve your goals more quickly and wonderfully. When

Tap into Your Thoughts

What do you imagine? Do you see yourself as wealthy? In a luxury car? In a beautiful home? In advanced stages of education and higher learning? In good grace and blessings? In comfort and life's beauty? If this is the case, then I commend you, because the secret and key to success and all of man's accomplishments truly is this. The world of existence obeys certain laws. Learn these laws and apply them. The type of people who learn and apply these laws are those who have amazing beliefs.

your goal is financial and you wish to become wealthy, you must search society and see who has achieved abundant wealth in a lawful manner and has become a successful individual. Then, consult with and make a role model of that individual, and learn from the person's valuable experiences, thereby traveling a journey of a hundred years in a single night.

Principle 13: Use the Power of Positive Imagination to Become Wealthy

You know that positive imagination and mental visualization send powerful commands to the subconscious. They say that the wealthiest of people are those who are able to imagine positively, more so and better than others. When you see wealth and financial power and its manifestations in your dreams, you can create that exact reality. The reverse is also true. Some people, those who possess negative thoughts, always see themselves in manifestations of poverty. They constantly think about the miseries of life and see themselves as failures.

Principle 14: Use Positive Affirmations

You know that a positive-emphasis sentence is a purpose-inspiring command to the subconscious mind. When you say, with a sense of power and hope, "I am a wealthy person," this powerful sentence is a command to your subconscious. This command can make a difference in your world, and consequently, the sentence that you have emphasized and affirmed can find realization in your life. This is the essence of positive-emphasis sentences.

Thus, always think about the manifestations and expressions of wealth and see yourself in a situation where those manifestations have been attained. Verbalize and affirm it. This method is one of the best ways to program your subconscious bio-computer.

Principle 15: Ask Wealth-Seeking Questions

If individuals ask themselves, "Why am I poor?" this question misleads the subconscious and causes it to create the conditions of a poor person for them, in terms of their mental and emotional state as well as their financial state.

On the other hand, if you constantly ask yourself, "How can I acquire lawful and abundant wealth?" the subconscious mind *emotionally* creates the conditions of a wealthy and happy individual in you and simultaneously searches the entire world of existence in order to see how it can actually achieve the conditions of a wealthy individual for you. That is why we previously mentioned that the quality of your life is determined by the quality of the questions you ask. So, wealth-seeking questions make you wealthy, especially questions that begin with the word *How*.

Remember that the questions you ask are commands for your subconscious mind. The type of questions that you usually ask yourself is very important. This is the secret to wealth and abundance.

Principle 16: Applying the Law of Gratitude

One of the most important principles of attracting wealth in life is to express gratitude towards God, the universe, other people, and yourself. This principle is also mentioned in the Quran, wherein God promises, "When you thank me, your blessings are increased." The Law of Gratitude states, "When you think about, and thank about, you bring about." So it is important that you always appreciate and be grateful toward God, other people, and even all of the parts of your body for providing you with health. This way, you can attract all kinds of wealth, including health, and live a life of bliss.

FINAL THOUGHTS

$\mathcal{W}$e have now come to end of this transformation-inspiring book. Your journey to success will be a long one and it will take work, but with the principles of the Technology of Thought, success and creating the life that you desire is within your reach.

Before we close this beautiful book, I have a few final thoughts. I have written you one final letter, which I hope will send signals to your subconscious mind one more time to deliver a message for lasting transformation. Read this letter with an open mind and open heart. Go to a secluded and quiet place so that no one can disturb you. Sit or lie comfortably and relaxed, and read on with complete tranquility.

Greetings, my good friends! Oh, fellow journeyers on the path of success, loyal followers of the Technology of Thought, wonderful students and oh, fellow travelers and musicians in life's beautiful concert.

In these moments, in which the extraordinary book *Think Yourself Successful* is seemingly coming to an end, I now sing melodies of hope and affection for you.

Together we will hum the exquisite, heartwarming anthem of happiness and success in this last stop on our journey.

Now, in these captivating and glorious moments, listen to my words with complete tranquility and contentment toward this amazing transformation. Your subconscious mind also listens and strengthens your beliefs as you constantly change and achieve excellence, peace, and beauty.

My words remind you that by living by the principles of the Technology of Thought, you have become an elegant, liberated, and serene individual and you live with complete tranquility and great self-esteem.

By concentrating on my words, you will become organized and programmed and will achieve an open and peaceful mind, smiling and content, and a completely wonderful feeling toward yourself and others.

Oh, successful students of the Technology of Thought, sit calmly in place and now listen to my words with absolute concentration and serenity. The words you read are the words of a friend.

I now ask of you to feel as though you are calm and free. I want you to pay attention to me, concentrate, and relax. At this moment, you are completely serene. You are listening to me, and all of your focus is on me. Allow all the exhaustion of your prior life to leave your body so that you become more and more relaxed every second.

Now take a deep, long breath in and a long breath out. Take another deep breath in and, as your body is calm, take another breath out. In this state, focus, and focus only on me.

You can now easily follow your friend's revelations of kindness and affection, and you are focused on nothing but my words. Words that give you peace and fill you with a passion for life.

You have now acquired a peaceful life. Celebrate it every day.

At this time, take a deep breath in, and with its exhale, release all exhaustion and tension out of your body. And now you feel comfortable.

In this moment in which you are relaxed, focus on the toes of your feet and loosen them up. This release and tranquility begins at your toes and encompasses your legs. It penetrates to your hands, and your arms feel rested, your shoulders are relaxed, and the calmness that began at your feet moves upward like a gentle wave.

Now loosen your feet. Your knees become loose and relaxed. This tranquility reaches your back. At this moment, your back is completely relaxed and calm. Loosen your hands and feel this tranquility and peace in your hands, feet, back, and chest.

Now, this wave of relaxation reaches your neck, face, and head.

At this moment, your head is relaxed. Your mind is calm. Your thoughts are tranquil. Your subconscious mind is at peace, and it confirms all the calmness of your body and sets out to build great beliefs in you.

Oh, fortunate and successful fellow traveler. Concentrate on yourself for a while. On the path of the Technology of Thought, see what you have done, how you have done it, the conditions under which you began this journey, and where you are now.

At a time when you were fed up with all of the failures, defeat, difficulties, and exhaustion or you were basically looking to find a better path for your life and livelihood, you were given glad tidings of success, fortune, and prosperity. And you came forth and, alongside a friend and hundreds of other good friends, you began a new journey in your life and achieved a great accomplishment.

Oh, successfully graduating student of the Technology of Thought. You broke free from your chains of pessimism, negativity, hatred, animosity, despair, and helplessness, and you started the engines of this powerful craft and are now ready to take flight.

My dear friend, you now possess the highest self-confidence. By receiving the best signals and positive messages from your thoughts and five senses, your sub-conscious mind has built the greatest self-confidence—the foundation of your beliefs—and now sets out to create the rest of the foundation of your sky-scraping and praiseworthy belief system.

Your subconscious mind executes all your commands, great captain.

You began the Technology of Thought with the Technology of Love, understanding the love from your creation.

You redefined yourself and everything became different for you. Filled with passion and emotion you cried out, "I am ready for this immense transformation!" And thus began our journey. On this journey, you achieved its foremost accomplishments: tranquility and a positive outlook. You know how to always keep your spirits high, and you understand how, at every moment, one must travel on the voyage of life with a happy, cheerful, and wonderful spirit using the power of concentration, the power of questions and thoughts.

My dear fellow traveler, on this journey you regarded your thoughts to be the main cause of your transformation, so you shut down the negative-thought-generating factory of your mind, and you only consistently used the factory that generated positive, ambitious, constructive, and morale-boosting thoughts.

Your subconscious mind, which, with all its endless power, is under your command, executes every one of your commands brilliantly.

With the commands, signals, and messages that it receives from you, your subconscious mind makes your body healthy, and for the rest of your life, so shall it remain. It will keep your figure fit, leave your countenance cheerful and elated, and make your smiles more and more beautiful.

Through the effective communication that you establish with your family, friends, loved ones, neighbors, and colleagues, you utilize the potential and capabilities of others. You and the other cherished beings, all of you sharing a single soul, are friends. Take advantage of this golden key and open all the doors of success for yourself, and create a masterpiece of your life. Turn every opportunity into a wealth, spread love, receive kindness, and live blissfully and happily.

Now, your goals and destiny are shaped by your own hands and are fulfilled through your own will.

My dear friend and fellow voyager, you see what an amazing feeling you have. You feel that in this environment, which is full of love, you think peacefully and brilliantly, and you pay attention to yourself and your subconscious mind.

The book *Think Yourself Successful* has been the book of your secrets, the secret to your success and the secret to your love. In this atmosphere, with this kind of thought system, you are always calm and you have a great feeling about yourself. You always feel a sense of your well-being, and your heart is filled with love. You have reached the belief that you are an amazing and successful human being, a creative graduate of the Technology of Thought, and a beautiful, transformed individual with a great character, who is completely captivating and kindhearted. You are an engaging and loving individual with a pleasant and bright face, a beautiful smile, and a peaceful and confident heart.

And now, my dear, with this wonderful feeling toward the book *Think Yourself Successful*, you have transformed with complete success. I commend you for choosing the right path in life and setting out to take advantage of all of your blessings and fortunes. Enjoy every moment of your life and live completely differently.

By applying the principles of the Technology of Thought, you have become a true human being. No longer are you ever alone; others are all your friends, who enjoy your companionship and company. At everything you do, you will be successful. Every experience for you is a beginning to greater successes. You attract people, and you are a magnet to wealth and riches. Based on the principle of self-awareness, at each moment you are attentive to yourself and your subconscious mind. You live majestically, magnificently, and with pride.

With the endless power of your subconscious mind, everything that you desire, you accomplish. For you, every day is different from the day before. Each day you achieve a new success and record it in your journal of successes.

Now, oh individuals transformed by the extraordinary book *Think Yourself Successful,* with complete pride and honor, open your lovely eyes, take a deep breath, and look at the beauty around you. Smile and say, "I have become successful, happy, and blessed, and I am beginning my new life alongside the Technology of Thought."

At this time, relax in your seat and allow us to experience these beautiful moments of togetherness for a little while longer.

I wish you a productive journey on earth. For the rest of our lives, which shall be long lifetimes of glory and health, we will remain deeply connected. Now move forward and continually think yourself successful.

NOTES

INTRODUCTION

1. Hajj is the holy pilgrimage to Mecca.
2. The Kaabah is a sacred cube-shaped building in Mecca.
3. From the Persian poet Mohammad Taghi Bahar.

CHAPTER 1

1. *Think and Grow Rich* is the book by Napoleon Hill that motivated me to make a change in my life and look toward a better future.
2. We received the equivalent of American food stamps.

CHAPTER 2

1. Quran 53:39 ("The Stars").

CHAPTER 3

1. Quran 45:13 ("The Kneeling").
2. From the book *How to Attract Money* by Joseph Murphy.
3. An Imam is a spiritual and religious leader. The word *Imam* is also used to denote a successor to the Islamic Prophet Muhammad, from the Shia Muslim viewpoint.
4. Imam Ali was the Prophet Muhammad's cousin.
5. Ferdowsi was a tenth-century Persian poet, renowned for his epic tale *Shahnameh* ("Book of Kings").
6. Hafez was a fourteenth-century Persian poet best known for his work *Divan*.
7. Rumi was a thirteenth-century Persian poet known for his works *Divane Shams* and *Masnavi*.
8. Jafar ibn Muhammad al-Sadiq was the sixth Shia religious leader.

CHAPTER 5

1. Quran 89:30 ("The Dawn").
2. Quran 3:159 ("The Family of Imran") and 42:38 ("The Consultation").
3. This is an Iranian expression that is used to reciprocate a compliment.
4. Quran 39:9 ("The Group").

5. Nezami Ganjavi was a twelfth-century Persian poet who is best known for his five long narrative poems *Five Treasures*.

CHAPTER 7

1. Abu Muslih bin Abdullah Shirazi, better known as Sadi, was a thirteenth-century Persian poet. He is most famous for his literary works *Bustan* ("The Orchard") and *Gulistan* ("The Rose Garden").

INDEX

ABOUT THE AUTHOR

*D*r. Alireza Azmandian was born in Tehran in 1953 to a religious family. He received his early education in Islamic schools, including Alavi High School in Tehran, from which he graduated at the top of his class in the field of mathematics. He obtained his bachelor's degree in mechanical engineering from the Sharif University of Technology in 1976. After his service in the army, which coincided with the victory of the Islamic Revolution of Iran, he became a successful television news reporter. As a result of reporting on the political and economic state of Iran and traveling throughout the country, as well as to many other countries, he gained a deeper understanding of the conditions of people's lives. Reporting from the battlefield during the Iran-Iraq War, he was able to present televised images of the war operations and to depict the courage, bravery, and selflessness of the Iranian soldiers.

After six years in television journalism, in order to pursue a higher education, he traveled to the United States in 1985 and acquired his master's degree in industrial and systems engineering with a concentration in engineering management. He also received his Ph.D. in industrial and systems engineering from the University of Southern California, at the same time teaching at U.S. universities.

Dr. Azmandian was appointed president of the Aftab Television Network in New York, striving for four years in that position to increase cultural opportunities for Iranians living in the United States.

During his twelve years of research and teaching at U.S. universities, Dr. Azmandian was able to do extensive scientific study on the capabilities of the mind, exchange views with researchers in this field, and attend scientific conferences on self-improvement and self-development. At the same time, he spent years researching and teaching to enhance this field, an important phenomenon of the new millennium. Dr. Azmandian returned to Iran in 1997 in order to pass on to his fellow Iranians the invaluable lessons of the self-development and self-management concepts he had learned, in a package he named the Technology of Thought.

While teaching as a faculty member of the Engineering Department at the University of Tehran, he founded the cultural-scientific institute of Padideh Fekr (the Phenomenon of Thought), and by offering "The Technology of Thought" classes, he continued to expand and advance this method in Iran. By creating enormous changes in the thought and belief systems of his students, he was able to completely transform their lives.

Professor Alireza Azmandian has traveled to more than fifty countries, including many in Europe, Asia, and Africa. He has studied the fundamentals of the mind and the infinite power of human thought and has acquired a deep understanding of the mechanisms of thought, beliefs, and programming the subconscious mind. Today, he uses his scientific achievements in the service of others, teaching that by utilizing the correct techniques of communication and the Technology of Thought, people can make positive fundamental changes in their thought system. Dr. Azmandian strives to create immense change in people's lives, inspiring them to become truly happy, cheerful, goal-driven, motivated, powerful, and determined human beings of high character, who have a complete sense of self-confidence and are filled with love and hope for an amazing and productive life.

Through conferences and Technology of Thought seminars for managers, university professors, industrial workers, teachers, students, company employees, and other influential figures of society, Dr. Azmandian has not only completely changed their thought system and mentality, but by using the techniques of thought management, he has also had an enormous impact on increasing their efficiency and ability to gain from human resources.

The success team members at the cultural-scientific institute of Padideh Fekr believe that by spreading this method among people and transforming the belief and thought system of each and every one of them, they are making an enormous contribution to the honor and greatness of society.